NEW IN CHESS
BOOKS

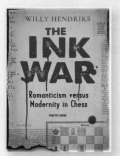

The Rivalry between Steinitz and Zukertort
Willy Hendriks

The rivalry between William Steinitz and Johannes Zukertort, the world's strongest chess players in the late nineteenth century, became so fierce that it was named 'The Ink War'. Who was the strongest player? And who had the best ideas? In *The Ink War*, IM Willy Hendriks once again offers his unique perspective on the birth of modern chess.

Another Hit Repert...
Christof Sielecki

Christof Sielecki prese... chess players of all leve... with the black pieces. W... safely navigate the open... ...understand what is happening and how you can play for a win. Yes, it is simple but not boring!

Training for Club Players (1800-2100)
Davorin Kuljasevic

The success of the book *How To Study Chess on Your Own* made clear that thousands of chess players want to improve their game. This Workbook gets you started immediately. Kuljasevic has used his coaching experience to create a broad and exciting training schedule.

Sharpen your endgame tactics
Thomas Willemze

In *1001 Chess Endgame Exercises for Beginners*, IM Thomas Willemze does two things simultaneously. He explains all the basic concepts and provides many exercises for each theme and each chess piece in a highly instructive puzzle rush.

The fourth volume of the *1001 Exercises* series.

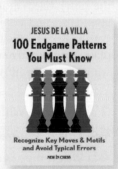

Chess.com 2022 Book of the Year
Ramesh RB

Coach Ramesh has won the *2022 Chess.com Book of the Year Award*, in a vote with thousands of chess players. It is well deserved. But beware! It is a tough book that will require some real effort. Are you up for the challenge?

"An absolute divine masterpiece" – *Andras Toth.*

Recognize Key Moves and Motifs in the Endgame and Avoid Typical Errors
Jesus de la Villa

If you liked the best-seller *100 Endgames You Must Know*, you will surely like this new book by the same author, a Spanish Grandmaster. Endgame patterns are crucial. They help you spot key moves quicker, analyze and calculate better and avoid making errors.

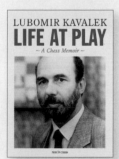

Kavalek's long-awaited memoir
Lubomir Kavalek

American-Czech Grandmaster Lubomir Kavalek (1943-2021) was a three-time US Chess Champion and one of the best chess writers of the last decades. Kavalek could speak from experience as he worked with or met all the chess greats of the last century, from Bobby Fischer to Nigel Short. Including many of his best games with Kavalek's entertaining comments.

A brilliant new endgame manual
Herman Grooten

The author of the bestsellers *Chess Strategy for Club Players* and *Attacking Chess for Club Players* finally explains how to play the endgame. He shows how to understand themes or patterns and for example tells you how to cut off the enemy king or create a passed pawn – and win many more endgames.

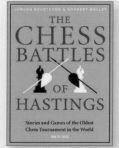

The oldest chess tournament in the world
Jürgen Brustkern & Norbert Wallet

No other chess tournament has such a long and rich history as Hastings. Countless chess players, professionals and amateurs alike, have celebrated Christmas and welcomed the New Year in Hastings while battling it out on the chessboard. The book covers the tournament's fascinating history and portrays forty of the most colourful participants. The stories begin in 1895 and span 125 years.

The updated classic with 100 extra pages
Mikhail Shereshevsky

In this widely acclaimed chess classic, Mikhail Shereshevsky explains how to master the most important endgame principles. Where other endgame manuals focus on the basics and theoretical endgames, this book teaches the 'big ideas' that will help you find the most promising and most practical moves in any endgame.

available at your local (chess)bookseller or at www.newinchess.com

2023 ISSUE 2

ENJOY THE BEST GAME. EVER.

NEW IN CHESS

10

'If you are fed up and don't want to prepare and you've got all these great talented youngsters who are super eager, it is not a given that Carlsen will stay number one forever'

(Anish Giri on page 51)

66

'What I would do if I could change one thing in the chess world? Erase engines.'

106

72

105

82

CONTRIBUTORS TO THIS ISSUE
Nodirbek Abdusattorov, James Altucher, Alexander Donchenko, Jorden van Foreest, Anish Giri, John Henderson, Peter Heine Nielsen, Maxim Notkin, Judit Polgar, Dimitri Reinderman, Matthew Sadler, Chad Smith, Jan Timman, Jonathan Tisdall, Thomas Willemze, Mustafa Yilmaz

PHOTOS AND ILLUSTRATIONS
Crystal Fuller, Jurriaan Hoefsmit, Lennart Ootes, Berend Vonk
COVER PHOTO New In Chess **COVER DESIGN** Hélène Bergmans

COLOPHON p.71
SUBSCRIPTIONS p.52

The Lost Tradition

A picture is worth a thousand words, so the adage goes, and in this one, taken in the 1980s by Boris Dolmatovsky, you can almost feel the anticipation from the large throng of fans squeezed tightly around Mikhail Tal's board. The 8th World Champion is playing Valentin Arbakov, a local grandmaster famous for his speed chess skills, in the Moscow Blitz Championship.

This was an annual summer outdoor event held at the Park of Culture museum, with the victor claiming the coveted prize of a Russian samovar. The 'samovar' tournament was one of the many tournaments seen as part of the rich chess heritage that was instilled in the Russian psyche and culture.

Sadly, with a year now passing since President Vladimir Putin's senseless war in Ukraine, sanctions are beginning to bite in Russia in all spheres. As grandmasters have left in large numbers, several commentators have begun to speculate that the war could also hit the Russian chess tradition and the future for their emerging stars. ■

Ye Olde Queen

London's Forum Auctions catalogue listings for January included a rare antiquarian 'chess' book. Lot 17 was *Summa Collationum*, written by 13th century Franciscan theologian John of Wales. The manuscript contains one of the earliest explana-

In his Summa Collationum Franciscan theologian John of Wales was critical of women and bishops.

tions for the rules of chess and also sheds light on a more humble – not to mention sexist – start to our game's most powerful piece.

Back in ye olde times, the queen could move only one space at a time in a diagonal direction. This 'aslant' style, explained Friar John, reflected the fact that 'women are so greedy they will take nothing except by rapine [violent seizure] and injustice'. And they are not the only pieces singled out for Friar John's prejudices. Bishops were deemed to 'move obliquely', he wrote, because 'nearly every bishop misuses his office for cupidity [avarice]'.

Fast forward a couple of centuries, and the game's only lady became all-powerful. Marilyn Yalom, the prolific feminist author and cultural historian, espoused the theory in her 2004 book, *Birth of the Chess Queen: A History*, that the modern queen's status on the chessboard can be dated to 15th century Spain during the reign of Isabella I, and reflected their growing power on the political stage.

With only two copies recorded since 1906, *Summa Collationum* was estimated to sell for between £18,000-22,000, but its hammer price only reached £16,000.

The Book Thief

The Herald newspaper in Scotland tells the charming story about a long-lost book that was stolen from Elgin Academy's school library nearly 70 years ago. Its mystery reader sent back a copy of Rev. E. E. Cunnington's *The Modern Chess Primer* from 1903. The small volume was now bound in elastic bands to stop the pages from falling out. He admitted in the accompanying letter that he 'stole' it from the Moray school in 1954, just to brush up on his chess skills during the summer holidays.

He went on to thank the library and the book's author for helping him in his quest of beating his classmates, before signing off as 'The Book Thief'. He also enclosed a £50 'contribution to 68 years of unpaid fees'.

Librarian Shelagh Toonen explained that with a late fee of 60p a week, the fine would have been

Librarian Shelagh Toonen with E.E. Cunnington's primer that was 'modern' in 1903.

£2,121, but the authority has a cap set at £10.40 and does not fine juniors or those aged over 60. The chess guide, costing three shillings and sixpence at the time and published by George Routledge and Sons Limited is now being kept as an 'archive' in the library.

The Queen's Gambit Declined

Lovers of Beth Harmon were thrown into a tizzy with speculation that a sequel was coming after actress Anya Taylor-Joy tweeted 'The Queen's Gambit 2'. The tweet was followed by an avalanche of likes and re-tweets, but the excitement soon turned to disappointment when it was revealed to be a hoax. Tipped off by Netflix, whose PR department went into meltdown after unexpectedly being inundated for release updates, Taylor-Joy moved to lock her account down and delete the tweet, as she explained

across her other social media platforms 'My Twitter has been hacked – apologies for all inconveniences, it's NOT me!'

Taylor-Joy's Twitter hack happened to come just as Anish Giri was finally emerging victorious at the Tata Steel Masters. No stranger to the subtle art of the deft tweet/retweet, the Dutch No1 just couldn't resist himself in victory by retweeting 'Think she tried stealing my thunder here'.

Dr Engine

We have all been amazed by the analytical powers of chess engines as they crunch millions of moves per second to make the best decision on the board. Now that brute calculating force is being trialled to see if it can make crucial decisions in the emergency room.

The man developing the idea is Adam DeHollander, an operations research PhD student at the University of Buffalo. 'I wondered if we could reprogram the algorithms that play chess to instead analyse the emergency department', says DeHollander in his university newspaper. 'Turns out you can basically convert the emergency department into a game and then use the algorithms to solve the game.'

A tournament chess player and volunteer chess coach, DeHollander got the idea for the game after a spell in the ER two summers ago, where he witnessed unnecessary overcrowding, wondering if a chess engine could do the job better. He started by simply converting a chess game into a virtual ER. The pieces on the board became resources like nurses and X-rays, while moves became decisions about allocating those resources.

The research, the subject of his doctoral dissertation, recently

Why wouldn't ambulances move like chess pieces?

received the 2022 Chessable Research Award. The award is for undergraduate and graduate students conducting any university-level research topic related to chess.

Dedicated follower of fashion

After he stormed up the world ranking to #2, many were puzzled about the sudden inactivity of Alireza Firouzja in recent months. The 18-year-old played very few tournaments, his last appearance since the Candidates being a brace of impressive back-to-back victories in St. Louis last July, winning the Rapid & Blitz and the Sinquefield Cup.

Many speculated that the Iranian-born teenager, who now plays for France, was in 'deep training' for a

Alireza Firouzja will be back, dressed to kill.

serious tilt at the World Championship title; but there were also rumours that he could well be about to embark on a couture career-change hoping to make his mark in the fashion industry. In a recent interview for Chess.com, Firouzja confirmed that it was indeed all true. 'Yes, I was in this [fashion] industry for two years now. It's kind of a serious thing. It's improving every day and, yes, it's kind of a real profession.' In the end he's hoping to have 'both things together' with a dual career. So there you have it: a world of catwalks and Catalans beckons for Alireza!

Little Man Tate

We've all watched in the media the spectacular car-crash downfall of the controversial self-proclaimed misogynistic influencer Andrew Tate. He was arrested and detained in Romania as a part of a human trafficking and rape investigation. And amidst the media feeding frenzy about Tate stories, chess has figured highly in several of them.

Tate – whose full name is Emory Andrew Tate – is the son of notorious IM Emory Tate. Many media stories have focused on the chess background of Tate Jr and his prowess at the board, several even wildly proclaiming him to be 'a chess genius'

or a 'chess prodigy'. When Emory died in 2015, we wrote in these pages of how he had to 'do constant battles with his inner demons' (Death of a Gunslinger, NIC 2016/1). There are several traits here that we also recognise in Andrew Tate's behaviour – someone who acknowledges his father to have been the biggest influence in his life and also his lifestyle coach and fitness coach.

Andrew did learn chess at a very young age from his father and was indeed a budding young chess prodigy, when at the age of 5 he attracted media attention by beating players in their mid-teens in American tournaments. His only other notably chess activity since then, though, has been online, reaching a rating peak on Chess.com of 1800 blitz, though his last blitz rating was around 1600. So certainly

Where there's smoke... Yes, Andrew Tate is a chess player.

he can 'play', but he's no chess genius as the media painted him.

Tate is seen in many videos and in media appearances playing chess or with a chess set in the shot. And the chess background certainly influenced the influencer! When his fleet of 32 supercars (remember he bragged to climate activist Greta Thunberg about their sizeable emissions?) were impounded by the Romanian authorities (karma, huh?), they were all housed in garages that had knight chess pieces motifs on them. ∎

Welcome back!

Large home crowd watches Anish Giri claim Tata Steel Masters

The Tata Steel Chess Festival celebrated the 85th jubilee edition with record attendance and a dream victory by Anish Giri. Finally, after five second places, the Dutch number one lifted the winner's trophy in Wijk aan Zee at 'the Wimbledon of Chess'.

NEW IN CHESS

by DIRK JAN TEN GEUZENDAM

At the bus stop right in front of the De Moriaan sports hall, the venue of the Tata Steel Chess Festival, visiting chess fans were welcomed with a friendly note asking for their understanding; an uncharacteristic warning that you do not expect to see at a chess tournament: Due to huge interest, the organizers pointed out, spectators might have to wait for a while before they could enter, particularly in the weekends.

As it was, there were queues most days, and that is not counting the growing number of well-informed autograph hunters waiting at the special entrance at the other end of the hall, where the grandmasters entered and left the building.

After two editions without amateur groups and spectators, the Tata Steel Festival resumed with a fully-fledged jubilee edition to celebrate 85 years of chess for everyone in Wijk aan Zee. Clearly it had been a long wait, as the fans turned up in record numbers. Hotels were fully booked, parking lots filled to capacity, restaurants and cafés were thriving and queuing was the new normal. In the café of De Moriaan there was a cap on the number of chess sets allowed, as the owner hoped to keep some tables for non-chess players. Everywhere you saw old friends meeting again, enthusiastically telling each other how wonderful it was to be back, and invigorating themselves with a warm bowl of the traditional pea soup.

NEW IN CHESS

Café De Zon was a popular haunt for chess fans of all ages.

At the end of the tournament, World Champion Magnus Carlsen, the most successful player in Wijk aan Zee history, expressed his disappointment about his result, saying 'I am kind of a little bit sick of (classical chess) after these two weeks'. With his growing aversion towards 'slow chess', he was a rare bird in Wijk aan Zee. Seldom before have we seen so many beaming faces, so many delighted fans and players, thoroughly enjoying the pleasures of a traditional chess tournament.

Welcome side effect

An additional reason for the queues were the tightened security measures. Visitors had to register online, and at their arrival they were checked. The use of telephones was not allowed, neither to make calls nor to take photos. Furthermore, the fight against cheating included a 15-minute delay of the live broadcast and the players were thoroughly frisked before entering the playing area. Fortunately for the audience and the press, the games could be followed live on the monitors in the hall and in the press room (but without evaluation bars or engine assessments!). A welcome side effect of this arrangement was that many players would come to the press room

again after their games had finished to watch the other games still in progress. And while they were there, they often had a look at their own game with their opponents instead of rushing back to the hotel to check their games with an engine, as had become common practice in recent pre-pandemic years. Inadvertently, the old habit of post-mortems was revived, much to the delight of the press representatives.

No Russians

With the usual mix of established stars and rapidly rising youngsters, the field was wildly attractive. The main absentees were the Russians, who were not welcome. The only Russian who came to Wijk aan Zee was FIDE president Arkady Dvorkovich, but he kept a low profile at the opening ceremony, leaving official duties to FIDE Vice-President Vishy Anand. The former World Champion and five-time winner received the first copy of a jubilee book and was guest of honour for a week.

The ban on Russian players robbed Ian Nepomniachtchi of a chance to warm up for the forthcoming World Championship match, an opportunity that his opponent, Ding Liren, welcomed now that he was no longer bothered by travel restrictions. Yet, the Chinese number one was unrecognizable. Uncharacteristically losing three games, he put up a poor performance and confessed that he had essentially lost motivation and interest in the tournament when, in the first week, the dates and venue of the match (April, Kazakhstan) had been announced.

NEW IN CHESS

Guest of honour Vishy Anand, FIDE Vice-President and the first ever Indian GM, with young stars Praggnanandhaa, Erigaisi, Adhiban and Gukesh at the opening ceremony.

Hotels were fully booked, parking lots filled to capacity, restaurants and cafés were thriving and queuing was the new normal

He was not the only one who underperformed or played a less prominent role than expected. Compared to most classical tournaments, the Tata Steel Masters and Challengers are unusually long in these days of shortened attention spans. Lasting 13 rounds, 'Wijk' has its own laws. Not only is the opposition formidable, the length of the contest puts extreme demands on perseverance and stamina. Just as in a marathon, it's not enough to run fast for 30 kilometres – you have to have reserve energy when your rivals start running out of steam.

Following their spectacular performance at the Chennai Olympiad, a lot was expected from the young Indian trio, Gukesh, Erigaisi and Praggnanandhaa. Pragg's result could hardly be called a disappointment, but Gukesh and Erigaisi had a rough time. The bright side, and further testimony to their exceptional talent, was that all three of them kept fighting till the very last moment and that every day the games that they were involved in contained a promise. With their typical modesty, they spoke about a great learning experience. It wasn't hard to see that underneath this controlled demeanour, there was a burning ambition to continue shooting for the stars.

Spectacular fireworks

As always, the top favourite was Magnus Carlsen, who was hoping to collect his ninth trophy. Likewise, the local fans once again kept their fingers crossed that finally the moment would come that Anish Giri would lift his first trophy. In the second round, the Dutchman gave the hopes of his followers a boost when he defeated Gukesh with spectacular fireworks.

NOTES BY
Anish Giri

Anish Giri
Gukesh D
Wijk aan Zee Masters 2023 (2)
Queen's Gambit Declined, Ragozin Defence

1.d4 ♘f6 2.c4 e6 3.♘f3 d5 4.♘c3 ♗b4 The Ragozin Defence, named after the Soviet grandmaster Viacheslav Ragozin (1908-1962).
5.♗g5 h6 6.♗xf6 ♕xf6 7.e3 0-0 8.♖c1

For this game against Gukesh, I had found an idea in a rather dusty old main line that seemed harmless compared to the trendier variations against the Ragozin.
8...dxc4 9.♗xc4 c5 10.0-0
This line is often played with the intention to simplify the game quickly, and I myself have played a couple of quick draws on the black side of this line. However, I discovered an unexpected new possibility, as you will see further on.

10...cxd4 11.♘e4 ♕e7 12.a3 ♗a5 13.exd4

I had had this structure with the black pieces in an old game against my coach Erwin l'Ami. Back then, Erwin was unable to create an initiative and I quickly took over thanks to long-term assets like the pawn structure and the bishop pair. Things were different then.
13...♖d8
A strong move, which didn't come as a surprise, as I had expected Gukesh to have prepared this far. Black is maintaining the flexibility of his queenside development, as it is sometimes important to play ...♗d7-c6 instead of the natural ...♘c6.

14.♖c2!?
An odd idea, which some engines place at the top of the list at a certain depth, but not with a very impressive assessment. It actually barely deviates from an unappealing 0.00 evaluation. In addition, the move doesn't look particularly smart, let alone good, and I was pretty certain it would come as a surprise to pretty much anyone. The reason I knew it might contain some venom is

because I was very familiar with the ♖c3-d3-rook lift idea, played by some of my friends from India. I knew it had to be taken seriously.

After 14.b4 ♗b6, 15.♖c3 doesn't quite work: 15...♗d7 16.♖d3 ♗c6 17.♖e1 ♗xe4 18.♖xe4 ♘d7, and Black has got a better version and equalized in Shyam-Lazarev, 2015: 19.d5 ♘f6! 20.♖e2 ♕c7!, unpinning and solving his issues just in time.

14...♗d7 This is the standard idea and something I had anticipated.

15.♖e2 The rook switches to the e-file, not the d-file.

15...♗c6 There are actually alternatives here, but this move is too natural.

16.♕c2!

A beautifully cunning idea, which I expected could come as a surprise, even if my opponent had spent time on the previous two moves. The subtle queen move actually prevents Black from developing the knight, since 16...♘d7? now loses to 17.d5! exd5 18.♘eg5!, with ♕h7+ coming. The standard 16...♗xe4 is also less tempting here, since after 17.♖xe4 ♘d7 18.d5 the desired response of 18...♘f6? (like in the Shyam-Lazarev 2015 game) loses to the 19.dxe6! sac.

16...♗b6?!

This is actually a deep move and a very understandable mistake. Black obviously assumed that ♖d1 would follow next, but then the ...♗xe4! operation would work much better due to the X-ray that the black d8-rook has on the d1-rook.

The engine also suggests the odd-looking 16...♖c8!?, and I also consid-

ered 16...♗d5, after which White gets a small advantage with the following sequence: 17.♗xd5 ♖xd5 18.b4 ♗b6 19.♘c3 ♖d6 20.d5!, making good use of the isolated pawn.

17.♖fe1!

Luckily, I resisted the urge to blitz out 17.♖fd1, and as I started calculating the lines, I suddenly realized that I had clicked through some of the lines in the morning before the game.

17...♔h8? 17...♗d5! was a sad necessity at this point: 18.♗xd5 ♖xd5 19.♘c3 ♖d6 20.d5 ♘d7 21.dxe6 ♖xe6 22.♖xe6 fxe6. I recollected seeing this variation earlier that day, which is how I realized that 17.♖fe1 must still have been in my notes.

17...♗xd4 allows an attack similar to that in the game: 18.♘eg5! hxg5 19.♖xe6!, and here, too, the complications work out in White's favour.

18.♘eg5!

It wasn't too hard to spot this, especially since this is the exact same response as what I had been planning against 17...♗xd4. A very pretty combination, but not exactly that of a creative genius.

18...hxg5 19.♖xe6! fxe6 20.♖xe6

White has sacrificed his knight to open the h-file and his rook to open the a2-g8 diagonal, and now the king on h8 is in a serious danger. Black has to give back the queen in order not to get mated.

20...♕xe6 Here 20...♕f7 21.♘xg5 ♕h5 22.♖h6+!! is probably not a relevant line, and there are a lot of other wins. But I liked this geometry.

21.♗xe6 ♗xf3

Here I decided to spend most of my remaining time to calculate a forced win, since it seemed very close already. But I couldn't quite get there, since Black seemed to always be able to give up the f3-bishop to deflect my queen, and the d8-rook for my e6-bishop, getting rid of the mating box. Still, that meant that I would regain more than enough material and be left with a massive advantage.

22.♕f5! This is the prettier move and it depends on the depth of the engine and the engine itself as to which of the two wins they prefer. The simple 22.gxf3 was also good.

After 22.gxf3 ♖e8 23.d5 ♘c6 24.♕g6 ♖xe6 25.dxe6 I thought this was going to be hard to convert, but the engine evaluation is quite clear here as well.

The 2023 Tata Steel Masters. Standing (l. to r.): Giri, Van Foreest, Gukesh, Keymer, Erigaisi, Carlsen, Aronian, Caruana and Maghsoodloo. Sitting: Ding Liren, So, Rapport, Praggnanandhaa and Abdusattorov.

22...♗e4 23.♕xe4

I hesitated a long time about which of the two options to go for, and finally I picked the right one.

The alternative 23.♕h3+!? is also a long forced sequence: 23...♔h7 24.♗f5 g6 25.♗xg6 ♖d7 26.♗xh7! (White appears to have achieved nothing, but suddenly we get to pick up the a8-rook, thanks to an efficient trip by the white queen) 26...♖xh7 27.♕c8+ ♔g7 28.♕xb7+ ♘d7! 29.♕xa8 ♘f6!, and I felt that Black would consolidate. Even though I am up material, I was really not sure how easy this would be to win, as Black will regain the d-pawn, activate his rook and try to target my f2-square.

Up to here the whole game must have been a very unpleasant experience for Gukesh, and now he quickly went for a move that loses quite trivially. There was still a way to fight on, though.

That way was 23...♖e8!. My opponent had seen this idea in the gxf3 line, but somehow forgot that it works here as well. He might have missed 24.♕xb7 ♘a6!.

After 23...♖e8, White continues 24.h4!. I had seen this tempting idea, but not the final point. Black has to prepare to return the exchange, as the threat of mate along the h-file is imminent (24.♕xb7 ♘a6 25.♕f7 ♖xe6 26.♕xe6, which was my main intention at this point, wouldn't have been that easy to convert against the best defence).

24...♘c6 (more resilient is 24...♘d7, and then sacrifice, but that doesn't look so tempting for Black either) 25.hxg5 ♖xe6 26.♕xe6 ♗xd4, and here I tried ideas of g6, ...♖d8, ♕h3+ ♔g8, ♕h7+, and they didn't quite work, so I gave up on this. Instead, there is a very elegant clincher, thanks to a very trivial geometry: 27.♕h3+! ♔g8 28.♕b3+! (somewhat unexpected, to be honest) 28...♔h8 29.♕xb7. The queen has really been working overtime.

24.♕f3!

Defending against ...♖d1 mate and threatening mate myself with ♕h5+.

24...g4 25.♕f8+ ♔h7

23...♖xd4?

ANALYSIS DIAGRAM

There were various ways to win, but I finally found the cleanest one.

26.♗f5+ ♚h6 27.♗c2!

The bishop protects against checkmate and also sets up a deadly finale, having moved out of the way. ♕h8+ and ♕f5 are deadly threats, so Black resigned.

The b8-knight and the a8-rook never got into the game from the opening. In the final position Black is still ahead materially, but it's absolutely hopeless.

■ ■ ■

The clash between Giri and Carlsen came as early as Round 4. The last and only time Giri beat Carlsen in a classical encounter was as long ago as 2011, when they were 16 and 20 years old. In the years that followed, Carlsen dominated their games, several times escaping and even winning when he took unwarranted risks. It was hard to predict what would happen this time. When Giri reached a highly promising position, the predictable reflex was to see how Carlsen would wriggle free. But that did not happen this time.

NOTES BY
Anish Giri

Anish Giri
Magnus Carlsen
Wijk aan Zee Masters 2023 (4)
Queen's Indian, Nimzowitsch Variation

1.d4 ♘f6 2.c4 e6 3.♘f3 b6

A minor surprise, although at this point, after having played Carlsen so often, it is really hard for him to impress me with a sub-line. The Queen's Indian Defence is in fact still a very respectable opening, even though it did get a reputational hit during the AlphaZero hype.

4.g3 ♗a6 5.♕c2!?

I was going to play a system that involves a sharp pawn sacrifice, but some of the lines weren't too fresh in my memory. Therefore I took quite some time to decide whether this was really the optimal choice. Recently, I have been more into the traditional main line with 5.b3.

5...♗b7 6.♗g2 c5 7.d5

This pawn sac is the point of the ♕c2 system. It was quite popular around the years 2008-2010, I believe, when the Queen's Indian was a more frequent guest in the practice of top players and I was making my first steps as a teenage theoretician.

7...exd5 8.cxd5 ♘xd5 9.0-0 ♗e7 10.♖d1 The main move, and from here on both sides can take some different directions.

10...♘c6

Another option is 10...♘c8, guarding the b7-bishop; but it has gone out of fashion somewhat.

11.♕f5!?

To surprise Carlsen, I had to surprise myself. Normally, I would opt for the much safer 11.♕a4, which leads to mass simplifications almost by force. However, a bunch of random arguments for 11.♕f5 had entered my head and I decided to go for that one instead. Truth be told, White is still very much in control here, too.

11...♘f6 12.e4

12...d6!?

This was already a serious surprise, even though it had suddenly occurred to me that I had analysed this system in great detail when preparing to secure my second GM norm in the last round of the Groningen Open in 2008. My recollections of the lines of 15 years ago were, frankly speaking, pretty hazy, but I did recall the pawn on d6, which even back then had me concerned.

12...g6 is the main direction of the theory: 13.♕f4 0-0 14.e5 ♘h5, and here White has a choice between different queen moves, with long-term compensation for the pawn, thanks to a very active position.

13.e5 ♕d7

The point of 12...d6!?. Black solves the issue of the hanging f6-knight by tactical means.

14.♕xd7+

I was certain that back in 2008 the theory was to go for the endgame, and I had no recollection of 14.♕c2, which over the board seemed like a much more fascinating option.

After 14.♕c2, the start of the line wasn't too hard to calculate, as the moves are kind of only moves: 14...♘b4 15.♕e2 ♗a6 16.♕e1 ♘c2 17.♕d2 ♘xa1 18.exf6 ♗xf6 19.♖e1+ ♗e7 20.♘c3 0-0-0. I believe I got this far, but assessing this seemed impossible, so I decided to pass.

14...♘xd7 15.exd6 ♗f6

Frankly, I was on my own here and I decided that, whatever was going on, I should start with some natural moves and see what happened, without overthinking things too much.

16.♖e1+!

An important inclusion. White's d6-pawn is not the main trump here; rather it is the fact that the h8-rook is not in the game for the time being.

16...♔f8 17.♘c3

I also considered 17.♘a3!?, trying

to avoid the ...♗xc3 structure, but I decided to go with the more normal-looking move.

17...♘b4

It is hard to call this move a mistake, since the engines approve of it and it is in fact still theory (there is even a correspondence game with it!). That said, I felt huge relief when this happened. I was much more concerned about the far more strategically complex option ...♗xc3!?, ruining my queenside pawn structure. After 17...♗xc3!? 18.bxc3 ♖e8, Black has to connect the rooks with ...f6 and ...♔f7 to take over the initiative, but it is not so easy with White having resources like ♘h4 or ♗h3 at some point: 19.♗f4 (19.♗d2 f6 20.♘h4 was what Carlsen suggested after the game and something I considered as well, but after 20...♘a5! Black gets to neutralize my light-squared bishop) 19...f6 20.♗h3!?

ANALYSIS DIAGRAM

and here Black has to make some passive move like 20...♗c8 or 20...♘cb8, with a roughly balanced position. Black has some long-term potential. For example, if we take the

rooks and light-squared bishops off the board, Black will have a technically winning endgame. But all these pieces are still there, and White can drum up counterplay while Black is trying to coordinate his forces.

18.♘e5!?

Deviating unknowingly from Carlsen-Pelletier 2008, a game I might have known back in 2008. I felt this was an excellent practical decision and was certain that White was now rolling free, thanks to the bishop pair and a flexible pawn structure on the queenside.

18...♘xe5 19.♗xb7 ♖d8 20.♖d1

Black has to work to win my weak d-pawn, and in the meantime White will try to push b4 and get more than enough compensation. That was sort of the general thought I had, and in the game it worked out perfectly.

20...♘c4

21.d7! The pawn is doomed, but it is not going down without a fight.

21...♘c2 Not a bad move, though played with the wrong idea.

The alternative would be 21...♔e7!?, which eventually led to a draw in a correspondence game from 2016, in

'I suspected I must have blundered some kind of tactic. I kept staring at the position and just couldn't see what it was'

which, after 22.♗c8 ♘c2 23.♖b1 ♘d6 24.♘d5+ ♔e6 25.♘xf6 gxf6 26.♗a6 ♖xd7, White was the one playing for the advantage, thanks to the potentially powerful bishop pair, but Black should hold with accurate play, in Verhaeren-Jørgensen, WS MN/144 email ICCF 2016, which Jørgensen did.

22.♖b1

22...♘d4? I had actually expected this, but at this point both of us were probably missing the same resource. The less intuitive but stronger move was 22...♘e5!. Black should keep the knight on c2 for now, preventing the b4 push. White has a few tempting and risk-free options, e.g. 23.♘b5!? or 23.♗e4 ♘d4 24.b4, but with accurate play Black should hold.

23.b4!

My intention when I played 18.♘e5 was to do something like 23.♗c8 ♘d6/♘e5 and 24.b4, which I assumed would lead to some kind of draw, with Black having to be accurate.

However, since I had plenty of time, I started considering alternatives and discovered, to my surprise, that there is more to this position. 23.♗d5 ♘e5

24.b4 was my next thought, but then 24...♘xd7! works. In the end, I realized that swapping the move order was the way.

23...♖xd7?

I was confused, because I really didn't see what Black was going to play after my next move, and I suspected I must have blundered some kind of tactic. I kept staring at the position and just couldn't see what it was.

Black had to pick up the d7-pawn with the knight, 23...♘e5!, trying to reinforce the c5-pawn. Here Black would be in pretty poor shape, as the c5-pawn is weak and the h8-rook still needs to join the game, but the game would be in full swing: 24.bxc5 bxc5 25.♔g2 ♘xd7 26.♘e4, and Black has an unpleasant position, but, unlike in the game, he is far from lost.

24.♗d5!

24...♘d6

Carlsen found what probably was the best practical chance, because it almost worked. I thought Black was dead lost and should have tried ...cxb4 and ...♘a5, when he at least collects a rook for two pieces: 24...cxb4 25.♖xb4 ♘a5 26.♖bxd4 ♗xd4

Twelve years after he pulled it off for the first time, Anish Giri scored his second classical win against Magnus Carlsen.

27.♖xd4. However, the problem for Black is that his position is so uncoordinated, that it will just lose by force. **25.bxc5 bxc5 26.♗a3 ♔e7**

Black is trying to get the rook into the game and is clearly not in time to do so. This seemed so winning that I relaxed somewhat.

27.♗xc5?!
What could be more natural. I had just made sure that 27...♖c8 was losing and decided not to waste any more time. Instead, it was a good moment to dig a little deeper and make sure the game would end swiftly.

The cleanest way was 27.♖e1+! ♔d8 (the point is that after 27...♘e6 there is 28.♘a4!, which is crushing) 28.♗xc5, and Black is utterly helpless. The h8-rook still can't enter the

game, White has already restored the material balance and the powerful bishops are raging.
27.♘a4!? was also better than the game.

27...♘e6!

I don't exactly know what I had missed. I think I had a blind spot for this move itself. I would assume there was a forced win here, but to my surprise I couldn't find one. That was really upsetting, but there was still a huge advantage left, so it was not the time to lament too much.

28.♗b4 I considered all the forcing moves and nothing seemed to work too clearly, so I finally decided to just keep it simple and try to win the game all over again.

On the one hand, 28.♘e4 ♘xc5 29.♘xc5

ANALYSIS DIAGRAM

was tempting, as White keeps the initiative. On the other hand, I didn't want to risk my long-term trump, the two bishops. If somehow White didn't win by force here, I was afraid of the prospect of a drawn opposite-coloured bishop ending: 29...♖c7 (after 29...♖dd8 30.♖d3 White's slow endgame attack is apparently deadly; 30...g6 31.♗c6 ♘f5 32.♘d7 ♘d4 33.♗b7 ♘xc6 34.♖e3+ ♔d6 35.♘xf6, winning) 30.♖e1+ ♔d8 31.♘a6! (these are tough resources to spot) 31...♖c8 (allowing White to win a pawn, but other squares are bad, too, for example after 31...♖c3 the computer just offers 32.♗b3!, claiming that Black will be unable to keep the position together) 32.♗xf7!. Beautifully done by the engine, winning a crucial pawn.

Test Your
Chess Trivia Knowledge

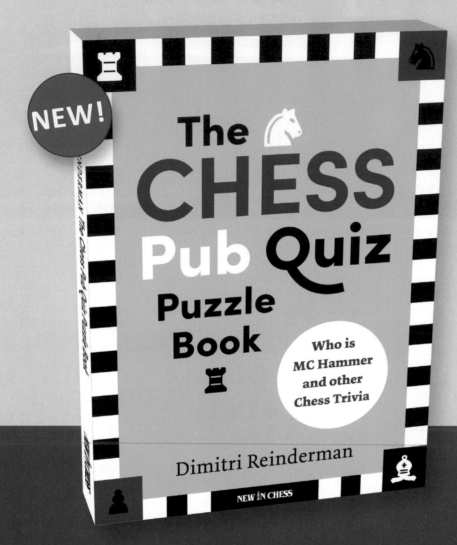

The most famous team ever participating in a chess pub quiz was MC Hammer. The team members are pretty decent chess players and happened to know their bit of chess trivia and chess history. Do you know or can you guess their names?

This book offers a collection of hundreds of chess trivia and chess-related trivia. You can use it by yourself, solving puzzles. Or you can use the book for multiple thematic pub quizzes at your local chess café or chess club.

144 pages | paperback €17.95 | available at your local (chess)bookseller or at newinchess.com | a **NEW IN CHESS** publication

28...a5?

Desperation, and also overlooking my strong 30th move.

I felt Black had a chance to get back into the game with 28...♗xc3 29.♗xc3 ♘f5, and I was really surprised that Magnus didn't grab that opportunity. The position probably remains technically winning, but that's how escapes from hopeless positions begin.

28...♗xc3 29.♗xc3 ♘f5! (I believe Carlsen may have missed this move, since after the game he mentioned 29...♖c8 30.♗b4! being the reason he didn't like the capture) 30.♗xe6!? I am not sure I would have found this concrete but very counter-intuitive idea. White wins a pawn by force, apparently (30.♗b3!?, and then trading all the rooks was what I thought was likely going to happen, and then I was really far from sure how easy it would be to convert such an endgame, given my slightly disturbed mood and the very special opposition) 30...♖xd1+ 31.♖xd1 ♔xe6 32.♖e1+ ♔d7 33.♗e5 ♘e7 34.♖g5 (the g7-pawn just falls) 34...♖c8 35.♗xg7 ♖g8 36.♗f6 ♖xg5 37.♗xg5, and this technical endgame arrives almost by force (31...fxe6 was an alternative, but would lose a pawn as well). Must be winning, but the engine evaluation is not decisive enough to be 100% certain about it. I guess it isn't too relevant anyway, since I would probably not look into the 30.♗xe6 capture that deeply.

29.♗xa5 ♖c8

Carlsen, with his exceptional feel for harmony, was relieved to have finally got his rook into the game, but the

price was rather high. Besides having the bishop pair, White is also a full pawn up now.

30.♘a4!

Not looking for an easy way out and pointing out that Black still has issues with his piece coordination. ♘b6 is looming and ♗b4, pinning the knight again, is a potential issue as well. All that, on top of White having a dangerous passed extra a-pawn that is supported by the d5-bishop, can do a lot of damage.

30...♘c4 31.♖bc1

It was tempting to give a check with ♗b4+ first, but this is even more unpleasant, creating more tension in Black's position. Here it was clear to me that, besides just being technically winning, I was probably winning by force here, due to all the pins and x-rays.

31...♗e5

Black is helpless and makes a waiting move. Remarkably, it almost worked, as I was considering to return the favour with the 'classy' 32.♔g2?? blunder 32...♘e3+! cheapo, which would give everything away. Luckily, I had already overlooked a resource

in this game once, and I was not keen on repeating the same mistake.

32.♗b4+ ♔f6 33.♘c5!

Forcing the win.

33...♘xc5 34.♖xc4 ♖dc7 35.♗a5!

Trading all rooks would lead to a technically won endgame, but this clinches it on the spot. Black is going to lose material due to the pin along the c-file after 35...♖d7 36.♗b6!.

I couldn't believe this was really going to happen, but having lost all hope, Carlsen resigned.

■ ■ ■

With this win, Giri took the lead, a position he shared with Nodirbek Abdusattorov, the leader of the Uzbekistan team that stunned friend and foe when they won gold at the Chennai Olympiad. In a short space of time, Abdusattorov has become a formidable force and it feels as if it's only a matter of time before he will enter the world's top-10. In Wijk aan Zee, he was accompanied by his mother and by his legendary countryman Rustam Kasimdzhanov, with whom he has been working in the past year.

Following the first free day, the Masters travelled to the Ajax football stadium in Amsterdam for Round 5. Abdusattorov, a big football fan and a supporter of PSG, had more than one reason to look forward to this excursion, since his opponent was Magnus Carlsen. It became another historic moment in the Uzbeki star's young career.

NOTES BY
Nodirbek Abdusattorov

Magnus Carlsen
Nodirbek Abdusattorov
Wijk aan Zee Masters 2023 (5)
English Opening

This game was played in Round 5, when the Tata Steel Chess Tournament travelled to the Ajax stadium in Amsterdam. It was my first classical game against Magnus Carlsen. I had prepared a lot of things on the rest day the day before, and I was extremely concentrated.

My approach was very straightforward. I had looked at his games, and he plays both 1.e4 and 1.d4, but before this game I had also looked at 1.c4. so I was ready for pretty much every first move.

1.c4 c5 2.♘f3 ♘f6 3.♘c3 ♘c6 4.e3 We are playing a classical symmetrical English Opening. I had mainly been expecting 4.d4 or 4.g3. According to the database, his most frequent choice has been 4.e3, but most of those games were played five or six years ago.

4...e5 But I had looked at 4.e3, too, and my memory was fresh when I went for this reply.

5.♗e2
The main line is 5.d4, as Magnus played in a game against MVL in the Grenke super-tournament in 2018, when he didn't get anything out of the opening. My plan was to play 5...exd4 6.exd4 d5, when Black is very solid and safe.

5...d5 The principled reaction.
6.cxd5 ♘xd5 7.0-0 ♗e7

8.♗b5
Honestly speaking, I had expected 8.d4. I was out of book now, but looking at the position, I thought it looked like a reversed Four Knights Sicilian in which White has spent two tempi on ♗e2 and ♗b5. I had played this with Black before, and I knew some ideas.
8...♘xc3 9.bxc3 ♕c7 10.d4 cxd4 11.cxd4 exd4 12.♘xd4 ♗d7

All this was very normal, but now a first surprise came.
13.♘f3
A very provocative move, which allows my reply.
During the game I had expected 13.♕c2, and my plan was 13...0-0, and now something like 14.♗d3 g6 15.♗b2 ♖ac8 16.♖ac1, which is maybe slightly better for White in a practical game, but looks pretty normal.
According to the engine, 13.a4 0-0 14.♗b2 ♖fd8 15.♕b1 was the best option and slightly better for White, but to the human eye it looks very equal.
13...♗f6!?

14.♗a3
The expected continuation, sacrificing the exchange. I had thought about this a bit, and had seen that I can castle queenside, and if my king gets to a8, it will be quite safe. I could not see much compensation for the exchange. The engine believes that the chances are equal, but in a practical game it's not so clear and I was quite optimistic about my chances, believing I might take over the initiative.
If White does not sacrifice the exchange, the position will be equal after 14.♖b1 0-0 15.♗b2 ♗xb2 16.♖xb2.
14...♗xa1 15.♕xa1 0-0-0 16.♖c1 ♔b8 17.♕xg7 ♖hg8
Here I was expecting 18.♕c3, but he played:

18.♕b2
Instead, the engine indicates that the only way to maintain equality was 18.♕xh7!, which looked very dangerous to me after 18...♗g4. But the cold-blooded engine gives 19.♗e2 ♗xf3 20.♗xf3 ♖h8 21.♕c2 ♕xh2+ 22.♔f1 ♖c8 23.♕b2, which is extremely unclear. But this is a line that is hard to come up with in a practical game.

18...♗g4! At this point I felt and knew that my position was far better.

19.♘e1

He thought for a long time about this move, spending something like 20 minutes.

I was expecting 19.♘d4 ♘xd4 20.exd4 (he cannot take my queen, 20.♖xc7 in view of 20...♘f3+, and he gets mated), when I was planning something like 20...♕b6 21.♗c5 ♕h6, with good attacking chances.

19...♖d1

Here I had a choice. I could go straight into the endgame with 19...♕e5, exchanging the queens, but then I realized that after 20.♗xc6 ♕xb2 21.♗xb2 bxc6 he can just go 22.♗d4 and hope to slowly squeeze me in the endgame. I believed he had good compensation, so I decided to exchange his active rook.

20.♖xd1 ♗xd1 21.♗f1

His only hope is to create counterplay on the kingside with his pawns. It is clear that White doesn't have enough compensation for the exchange, but here I made a mistake. My main problem is how to reorganize my pieces and to get my queenside pawns moving. With my next move

'The engine believes that the chances are equal, but I was quite optimistic'

For Round 5 the Masters went 'on tour' to the Ajax stadium in Amsterdam, where Nodirbek Abdusattorov ground down World Champion Magnus Carlsen in an epic battle.

I thought I threatened ...♘g4, or ...♘f3+, to swap his knight, thinking this was very strong.

21...♘e5?!

The engine says that 21...♗g4 22.♕f6 ♗e6 and stabilizing the position was clearly better, and only then ...♘e5 and ...♘g4, which it believes would be winning, even though it would require some accuracy on Black's part.

22.h3 Around here, we were getting low on time. For the remaining 18 moves we had only 20 minutes left, and one of our main problems was time management.

22...♗f3

Planning to bring back the bishop to d5 or c6.

23.♕d4

An understandable decision.

However, according to the engine, 23.♕b1! was very strong. Once you know it's strong, it looks easy, since it targets h7. But all in all it is not an easy move to find, because its real strength is shown in a sub line. I have to play 23...♗d5 (the real point is revealed after 23...f6, which seems to hold Black's position together, but after 24.♕b3! ♖g6 25.♕e6 White actually wins!), and after 24.♕xh7 he gets the pawn for free and the situation is very unclear.

23...♖d8 24.♕h4 ♗d5 25.♕xh7

25...♗c4

Here I had the choice between immediately taking the a2-pawn and forcing the bishop swap. I chose the latter, since it robs him of the bishop pair and eliminates a defender.

26.♗b2 ♗xf1 27.♔xf1 ♕c4+

28.♔g1 ♘c6

At this point, we were both down to about 10 minutes.

29.♘f3 ♕xa2 30.♗f6 ♖d1+ 31.♔h2 a5

Basically it's now all about the passed pawns. He will try to push his h-pawn and I will try to queen my a-pawn. I had the feeling that I had messed up earlier on and was slightly disappointed, but I still believed I had chances to win this game.

32.♘d4 ♕d5

Bringing the queen to the defence.

33.♕c2

Trying to trap my rook.

33...♕d6+

I decided to go for the queen ending. It felt like a logical decision in time-trouble, because although it might reduce my chances, it was risk-free.

34.f4

Pretty much forced.

34...♖xd4 35.♗xd4 ♘xd4 36.exd4 ♕xf4+ 37.g3 ♕xd4

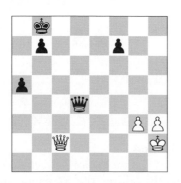

When I went for this, I believed my chances of winning or drawing this were 50-50, but at least I ran no risk of losing, and I could continue playing

this for another 100 moves or so. As it was, it took only 22.

38.h4 a4 39.♕a2 f5 40.h5 ♕h8

41.♕xa4

We had made the time-control, the h- and a-pawns are traded and we get a queen ending with b- and f-pawns against g-pawn. According to the table bases, it is a draw, but in a practical game it is hard to defend for White.

Taking on a4 was inaccurate, but I think he was not sure about going 41.♕f7, which looks very dangerous and requires a lot of calculation, but in the end it would have been easier for White to play this way: after 41...a3 42.♕xf5 ♕b2+ 43.♔h3 a2 44.♕f8+ ♔a7 45.♕c5+ I don't think I would have been able to hide my king from his checks and it would have been an easier draw. But this was very hard to see during the game.

41...♕xh5+ 42.♔g1

Queen endings are rarer than rook endings and you tend not to spend as much time on them. But I knew the main principles of this endgame. For instance, if White manages to trade his pawn against my f-pawn, it's a

draw. Recently I had the opportunity to follow the endgame between Gukesh and Mamedyarov at the Gashimov Memorial. In that rapid game, Gukesh held with a pawn less, and I had fresh memories from that game.

42...♕f3 43.♔h2?

Apparently, this is the decisive mistake.

I thought that after 43.♕e8+! I would be able to improve my king's position and that after 43...♔c7 44.♕e5+ ♔c6 45.♕e6+ ♔c5 46.♕e5+ ♕d5 my king would hide somewhere; but according to the table base, he would continue to check my king, and it would be a draw: after 47.♕c3+ ♔d6 48.♕f6+ ♔d7 49.♕g7+ there is nowhere for my king to run and hide.

43...♕e2+ 44.♔g1 ♕e5!

Now I am winning. My queen is on the ideal central square, from where it controls a lot of crucial squares and also prevents his king from walking over to the queenside.

45.♔f2 b5 46.♕b4 ♔b7 47.g4

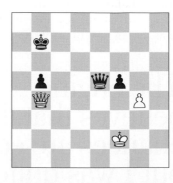

He manages to trade his g-pawn for my f-pawn, but the position is lost because my queen is perfectly placed and his king is not. It's also crucial that his king is not on g8 or h7, because that would be the ideal square for the king to be when my pawn reaches b2, as he could give checks with his queen from the first and second rank and I would be unable to exchange the queens. The rest is a pretty easy win for Black.

47...fxg4 48.♕xg4 ♔b6 49.♕g8 b4 50.♔f3 ♔b5 51.♔g2 ♕e2+ 52.♔g3 ♕e3+ 53.♔g2 b3 54.♕b8+ ♔c4 55.♕g8+ ♔c3 56.♕c8+ ♔d2 57.♕h8 ♔c2 58.♕c8+ ♔d1 59.♕h8 ♕d2+ 60.♔g3 b2

White resigned.

■ ■ ■

Losing a classical game is something that doesn't happen too often to Magnus Carlsen, and losing two in a row is clearly a rare anomaly. The last time he lost two consecutive games was almost eight years ago, in 2015, when he started Norway Chess with two zeroes.

This second loss left the World Champion two points adrift of the sole leader Abdusattorov, who made a very solid and eager impression. But as said, it's an unusually long event, and you didn't have to be a psychologist to suspect Magnus Carlsen of seeing a challenge in his seemingly hopeless position.

In the next few rounds, Abdusattorov kept dominating, and when the players enjoyed their second rest day after eight rounds, the Uzbeki was leading majestically, a full point

ahead of Giri and Wesley So. Carlsen was still one and a half points behind, but in Round 8 he won a game as Black that he had not counted on when Fabiano Caruana ruined his tournament with a losing blunder. It proved to be a decisive moment for the American, who had been playing well, but failed to create anything, as he put it himself, in the remaining games.

That Carlsen was still thinking about pulling off the impossible became clear after the game against Caruana, when he explained that it would be unrealistic to speculate about his chances, but that on the other hand he still had 'five winnable games' left. In the end he only won two of those, but in hindsight it is true that he only spoiled his chance to finish first in the penultimate round, when he missed a winning chance against Praggnanandhaa that understandably robbed the World Champion of his sleep.

Magnus Carlsen
Rameshbabu Praggnanandhaa
Wijk aan Zee Masters 2023 (12)

position after 21...♖e8

22.♖fe1?
Missing a chance to get a winning advantage with a neat tactic: 22.♘xf7 ♔xf7 (if Black doesn't take the knight, White will just withdraw it and be a healthy pawn up) 23.♖f3! ♕d7 24.♕d3, and Black's position is pretty hopeless. After the game continuation Black was only slightly worse, and the players agreed on a draw on move 67.

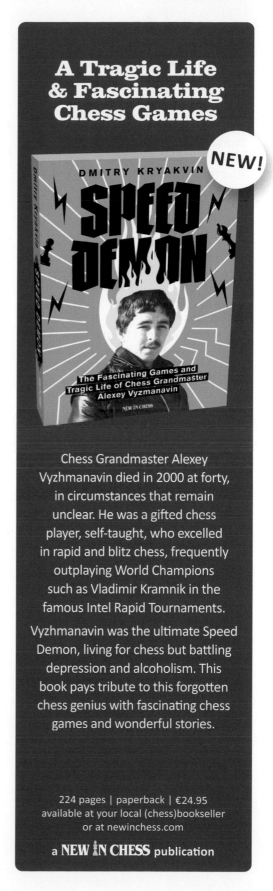

Historical final weekend

Abdusattorov continued to lead, and his main rival had become Anish Giri. In Round 9 both had the kind of luck you need to score a major victory. Abdusattorov survived a lost rook ending against Vincent Keymer (see Jan Timman's column) and Giri won an up and down game against Ding Liren after the Dutchman had been in trouble in the opening.

After their game in Round 11 had ended in a draw, Abdusattorov entered the final weekend half a point ahead of Giri and a full point ahead of Carlsen and So. That final weekend will go down in Tata Steel chess history as an absolute thriller and will not easily be forgotten by the Dutch fans.

A major role was played by Jorden van Foreest, who had demonstrated that he knows from experience how long the tournament is and that giving

Van Foreest joked: 'I'm just excited to play the role of spoiler and try my best to ruin some tournaments!'

up is never an option. In the first half, the winner of the 2021 edition lost no fewer than three games, but gritting his teeth he kept looking for his chances and regained confidence with a fine win against Erigaisi.

As fate would have it, Van Foreest was paired against both Giri and Abdusattorov in the last two rounds. As if he felt what was coming he joked on Friday: 'I'm just excited to play the role of spoiler and try my best to ruin some tournaments!'

On Saturday, Abdusattorov fairly comfortably drew as Black against Wesley So, while Carlsen missed a golden chance against Pragg as sketched above. The battle of the day was the clash between the Dutch numbers two and one.

NOTES BY
Jorden van Foreest

Jorden van Foreest
Anish Giri
Wijk aan Zee Masters 2023 (12)
Queen's Gambit Declined, Ragozin Defence

1.d4 ♘f6 2.c4 e6 3.♘f3 d5 4.cxd5
I was hoping this would come as a slight surprise for Anish, as I had not played this before. At the same time, the idea of a quick cxd5 is quite popular at the highest level, so I was sure it would not entirely catch him off-guard.

4...exd5 5.♘c3 ♗b4
I thought Anish might do this: transposing back to the Ragozin Defence. The most common way of playing is 5...c6, when Black has a comfortable Carlsbad, but at least all the pieces are on the board and an interesting game lies ahead. The game Carlsen-Nepomniachtchi from the 2022 Sinquefield Cup was a nice example of how things can play out in White's favour.

6.♗f4 ♘e4 7.♖c1 ♘c6
The most topical line, although Black does have alternatives, e.g. 7...♘d7, which was played by Gukesh in his game versus Carlsen in the same tournament.

8.h4!?
I don't know whether to give this move an 'interesting' sign or a 'dubious' one. Objectively, the idea is certainly not great, but I could not resist the temptation of going for it. In many lines, Black's idea is to play for ...g5, and this move is an attempt to stopping this. Doing so comes at

a serious price, however, as we will soon see.

8...♗f5 9.e3 White simply cannot do without this move.
9...♘xc3 10.bxc3 ♗a3 Yes, this wins a full exchange for Black!
11.♖b1 ♗xb1 12.♕xb1

White has lost the exchange as early as move 12. Certainly not great, you would think. Yet, there is some serious compensation, since Black's pieces are not coordinating particularly well and the rooks are not in the game yet. Moreover, White might be able to launch an attack fairly quickly in case Black castles, using the ♘g5 jump.

12...♖b8 Probably not the best way, but a very human one, just protecting the attacked pawn.

13.♕b3 ♗d6
Anish thought about this one for a while, thinking he'd calculated a way to a forced draw. Although this gives up the d5-pawn, the position is simplified a bit and White needs to spend some tempi with the queen.

13...♗e7 was another interesting alternative – hanging on to the pawn – that the reader might want to investigate.

14.♕xd5 ♗xf4 15.♕e4+

Using this clever intermediate check, White can regain the bishop while keeping a fluid pawn structure.

15...♕e7 16.♕xf4 ♕a3

It is this queen sortie that formed the start of Anish's idea.

17.♕e4+ ♘e7 18.♕c2 ♘d5

Anish had calculated this far, thinking that move repetition with 19.♕e4+ ♘e7 20.♕c2, etc., would now occur. I was not ready to agree to a draw so early, though.

Jorden van Foreest did not lose heart when he lost three games in the first half. With fearless and uncompromising chess he played a key role in the sensational last rounds.

19.c4!?

As it turns out, White can continue the game in this fashion. I did not know much more than that the computer evaluated this as 0.00, but I was already happy enough to get an interesting unbalanced game.

19...♘c3?!

This was a slight surprise, as it seemed to me that going for the endgame would have been a more practical decision.

After 19...♘c3+ 20.♔d1! ♕xc2+ 21.♔xc2 ♘f6, although Black is up an exchange for a bishop and pawn, to me the position seems slightly better for White from a practical point of view. His pawn centre is really strong and it is not easy for Black to activate his rooks. Yet, I did expect Anish to go for this, as things can never be all that bad.

20.c5!

It is important to create a square for the bishop on c4. At the same time, Black's queen and knight suddenly feel detached from the rest of the board.

20...b6?!

The first objective inaccuracy. Understandably, Anish wanted to break up the pawn chain but now his king will come under a fierce attack.

The engine recommendation is 20...♘xa2, although I prefer White here as well after 21.♗b5+ c6 22.0-0 cxb5 23.♖a1!. I had seen this line during the game and was quite satisfied, as the knight is regained and White retains a strong pawn chain from f2 to c5. Still, after 23...♕a6, followed by 24...♕g6, Black is probably not doing all that badly.

21.♗c4 bxc5 22.0-0 0-0 23.h5!

I quickly saw this move and immediately understood that things were suddenly extremely dangerous for Black, the point being that the immediate 23.♘g5 can still be met strongly by 23...g6, but now ♘g5 is an actual winning threat.

23...♕b4?

Under pressure both on the board and on the clock, Anish makes a losing error.

Instead, 23...♖b4, the same square but the other piece, would have kept Black in the game! 24.♘g5 g6 25.hxg6 ♖xc4 26.g7 ♔xg7 27.♕xh7+ ♔f6 28.♕h6+ ♔e7 29.♘h7. This is certainly no fun for Black, but amazingly, according to Stockfish, he would be okay after both 29...♖h8 or 29...♖d8.

23...h6 stops ♘f5, but allows other means of attack. 24.♗f5!. The bishop is ready to form a battery with the queen from d3, with a decisive result. **24.♘g5 g6 25.♕d3!**

Here I understood that I should be

winning. Black's queen and knight are completely out of the game, and the attack seems to have only gained in strength.

25...♖b6!

The most resourceful defence. I have to mention that from this point right up to the end of the game, Anish was extremely resourceful, finding one clever idea after another.

26.dxc5?

A serious mistake. I had spent quite some time, but could not figure things out entirely and overlooked a quite simple defence. Soon after making my move, I understood that 26.♖c1 should have been winning. The knight on c3 was providing Black with some tricks in some lines, but by first kicking it away to a4, White eliminates those tricks from the position.

After 26.♖c1! ♘a4, 27.♕e4! is the real killer, as the multitude of threats such as ♗xf7+ or ♘xf7, or even ♕h4, are simply unstoppable.

26...♖c6

27.hxg6

Having noticed that plan A was not working, I decided to switch to plan B. When going for my 26th move, I thought 27.♘xf7 ♖xf7 28.h6 would win on the spot, only to find I had missed a crucial detail: 28...♕xc5 29.♕d8+ ♕f8 30.♗xf7+ ♔xf7 31.♕d7+, picking up the rook, and winning the game I thought. But a cold shower was awaiting White in the end: 31...♕e7 32.♕xc6 ♘e2+! 33.♔h1 ♕h4, mate.

27...♖xg6

28.f4

For a moment I thought I had spotted a win with 28.♘xf7, but once again I found an amazing resource for Black: 28...♖xf7 29.♖c1 ♕b7!, creating a sudden counterattack on the g2-pawn, which saves the day.

28...♖g7?!

I thought this was another good move, which overprotects both the f7- and the h7-pawns. However, as it turned out, this was another losing mistake.

28...c6, with the idea of bringing the knight back to d5, seems to hold the balance, but such moves are not that easy for us mere mortals to spot.

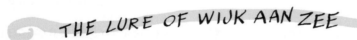

THE LURE OF WIJK AAN ZEE

I LOVE THE SMELL OF PEA SOUP IN THE OPENING!

BEREND VONK

way to advance them at all. There is now the simple idea of playing ♔f4, removing the bishop, and playing e4-e5, which is quite dangerous.

41...♔g7 42.♔f4 ♖a3
Around here, Anish started spending lots of time. While White's play is quite easy, it is not at all clear how Black should approach the situation. Clearly, the passed a-pawn is a serious asset, but it will not be easy to queen it. Instead, he starts playing to stop my plans, but as we will see, this is not so easy.

43.♖d4

29.♖c1?! Missing a second win, although this one was a lot harder to find than the first one.

After 29.♘xf7 ♖gxf7 30.♔h2!, it turns out that although White is a rook down, there is no reason to rush. By removing the king from the first rank, the crushing ♖f3 is prepared without allowing ...♕b1+. Black simply has no defence against this.

29...♘a4

An excellent find, as he prepares ... f5 to drive away my central knight.

33.♖b1 ♘d3 34.♖c2 f5 35.♗xd3 fxe4 36.♗xe4 ♖e7 37.♖b4 ♖d8!

In this way Black generates enough activity with the rooks for equality.

38.♔f2 A sharp decision, giving up a pawn, but activating the king in the process. It was also possible to play it more safely, but I still felt I might have winning chances in the ensuing endgame.

38...♖d2+ 39.♔f3 ♖xa2 40.g4 h6!

30.♘e4?
I was getting rattled by my failure to find a win, and was spending a lot of time. In the end, I decided to involve the knight. Although this did not feel good, I did simply not see how to continue and decided to play it safe instead.

30.♘xf7! was still good, but the complications are hard to evaluate for the human brain: 30...♖gxf7 31.a3! (a nasty move, forcing Black's queen away) 31...♕b2 32.♗xf7+ ♖xf7 33.♖c4, and the knight on a4 is picked up and White is still doing very well.

30...♘b2 31.♕b3
Going for the endgame, where I hoped I could perhaps push a little due to Black's awkward knight on b2.

31...♕xb3 32.♗xb3 ♔h8!

It is important to hinder the progress of White's passed pawns as much as possible.

41.f5 At first I did not like putting my pawns on light squares, but I soon understood that this would be the only

43...♔f6 The logical choice was 43...♖c3, but strangely enough, the c5-pawn is not all that relevant to the position: 44.♗d3 ♖xc5 45.e4. Black is back to being up a full exchange, but White's pawn mass is quite dangerous.

44.♗d3 Clearing the way for the e-pawn.

44...♖a2 A smart idea, since Black will now be able to check the white king. Ideally, the white bishop would be on f3 to stop these checks, but that would have left the e3-pawn hanging.

45.e4 ♖f2+ 46.♔e3 ♖g2 47.♔f3 ♖d2

For a moment, I was about to repeat moves here with 48.♔e3, but then I decided to keep this interesting game going and see what happened.

48.♖d8

Hinting at some ♖f8+ or even ♖g8 ideas to disturb Black's king.

48...♔e5

This one surprised me quite a bit, as I felt that I could now play ♖d5+ at any time, whenever it suited my plans.

49.♔e3 ♖g2

In a perfect world, White would have liked to play 50.♗e2 here, intending to achieve the ideal set-up of ♗f3 and ♔f4 in the long run. However, for now, Black can conveniently meet this with 50...♖xe2+, simplifying to a drawn rook ending. Looking for ways to continue the game, I spotted one last try.

50.♔f3 ♖d2 51.c6!

Creating the idea of ♖d7...

51...a5 52.♔e3 ♖g2 53.♗e2!

Finally this is playable under more favourable circumstances, as the rook ending after 53...♖xe2+ is no longer so simple.

53...♔f6

After 53...♖xe2+ 54.♔xe2 ♔xe4 I have 55.♖d7!. It was for this reason that I played 51.c6. After 55...♖e8 it turns out that Black is still able to make a draw, but it looks awfully scary in a practical game: 56.♖xc7 ♔d5+ 57.♔f3, and now 57...♖a8! is the only move to make the draw! Black has enough counterplay with the a-pawn.

54.♗f3 ♖c2 55.♔f4

White has finally achieved the perfect set-up, which means that Black needs

to start pushing his a-pawn quickly in search of counterplay in order not to be run over by White's pawns.

55...a4 56.♖g8 Creating the threat of e5, or so I thought.

56...a3!

Somehow I had totally missed that Black can in fact allow 57.e5+, and I wondered for a second whether I would lose now.

57.♖f8+

It would have been smarter to play this on the previous move, but fortunately nothing has been ruined. After 57.e5+ ♖xe5 58.♖g6+ ♔e7 59.♔xe5 a2 Black queens with check and wins the game.

57...♔g7 58.♖a8

58...a2

It is so natural to push the pawn that I did not even consider 58...♖c3, but it is actually a draw anyway: 59.e5 ♖xf3+! 60.♔xf3 ♖xe5 61.♖xa3 ♖c5; after the exchanges we have reached a dead-drawn rook ending.

59.e5 ♖e8! Bringing the rook back in the game just in time!

60.♖a7 ♔f8 61.e6

It would be desirable to play 61.f6, keeping the pawns on dark squares,

but then there would have been 61...♖c5 in reply, picking up the e-pawn.

61...♖f2

Under no circumstances can the white king be allowed to enter the black camp to f6. Although the position is tricky to play for Black, Anish defends it like an absolute machine.

62.♔g3

Slightly strange, but I had a concrete idea in mind.

62...♖d2

63.♔f4

63.g5 had been my idea, clearing the h5-square for the bishop, and I was about to play it when I stumbled upon a stunning refutation: 63...♔e7!. It is vital to activate the king, even at the cost of a pawn: 64.♖xc7+ ♔d6 65.♖d7+ ♔c5! (as 65...♔e5 runs into 66.♖xd2 a1♕ 67.♖d5 mate!) 66.♖a7 ♔b6. I spent some time evaluating this position, but finally concluded that Black is doing alright here with his activated king and his remaining a-pawn.

63...♖f2 64.♔e3

Since the ♔g3 plan did not quite

work out, I decided to try and activate the king in a different way and slowly bring it to e5.

64...♖b2 65.♔d4

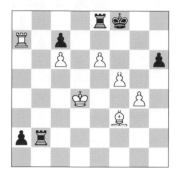

65...♔g7!

Once again Anish proves up to the task. After this last hard decision the game quickly fizzles out to a draw. 65...♔e7 would be the logical way of activating the king, but this does not work: 66.♔e5! ♖b5+ 67.♗d5 ♖d8 68.f6+ ♔e8 69.f7+ ♔f8 70.♔f6, and Black will be checkmated.

66.♖xc7+ ♔f6 67.♖f7+ ♔g5 68.♖a7 ♖d8+ 69.♔c3 ♖f2 70.♔e4 ♖e2 71.♗c2 ♖d6

Forcing the exchange of the a-pawn for the c6-pawn.

72.♖xa2 ♖xc6+ 73.♔d3 ♖h2

Since White is rather awkwardly pinned along the second rank, it's time to look for a forced draw.

74.e7 ♖c8 75.♖a6

I spent a few minutes and concluded that this forces the draw.

75...♖cxc2 76.e8♕ ♖hd2+ 77.♔e3 ♖e2+ 78.♔d3 ♖ed2+ 79.♔e3 ♖e2+

Draw.

■ ■ ■

And so, after the dust had settled, Abdusattorov began the final round leading with 8 from 12, half a point ahead of Giri and one point ahead of Carlsen and So, who could only hope that the leaders would falter. While So made a draw with the black pieces against Praggnanandhaa, Carlsen set to work to fight for his very last chance.

NOTES BY
Peter Heine Nielsen

**Arjun Erigaisi
Magnus Carlsen**
Wijk aan Zee Masters 2023 (13)
King's Indian Defence

The situation before the last round was clear. Magnus needed to win in order to have any chance of winning the tournament at all, as he was trailing Abdusattorov by a full point. Having the black pieces is generally not seen as ideal in such a scenario, but it is noteworthy that, this year in Wijk aan Zee, Magnus managed to win as many as four games as Black!

1.♘f3 ♘f6 2.g3

In a way a brave choice, just aiming to play chess rather than trying to force events by following long theoretical lines. While the young Indian's tournament took a turn for the worse in the latter half, his spirit for fighting chess always seemed to be there.

2...b6 3.♗g2 ♗b7 4.0-0 g6!?

The double fianchetto in this manner is a rather rare guest at top level. The

main reason is that it only arises logically via the 1.♘f3 move-order, as after 1.d4 ♘f6 2.c4 Black kind of has to play 2...e6 before going 3...b6 for a regular Queen's Indian. Perhaps for that reason, the double fianchetto has not gained much attention, but in Sergey Tiviakov's recent *Rock Solid Chess*, the Dutch grandmaster gives an excellent overview of the strategical concept of the opening by

'While Erigaisi's tournament took a turn for the worse in the latter half, his spirit for fighting chess always seemed to be there'

showing a number of his own games in the line. In such an inspiring way, apparently, that even the World Champion decided to give it a try!

5.c4 ♗g7 6.d4 0-0

7.d5!? One of the charming aspects of the system is that is already not so obvious here how White should react. 7.♘c3 may look like the logical move, but 7...♘e4 just leads to favourable exchanges for Black, and unlike in the regular Queen's Indian, Black, as a bonus, opens the long diagonal, with easy equality.

Apart from the game move, 7.♖e1 is another critical move, played by Nakamura against Magnus in a later online game. Then it becomes a typical 'waiting game', as after 7...e6 8.♗f4 d6 White avoids playing ♘c3, not allowing ...♘e4. But here it is somehow White who runs out of useful moves first. 9.♕c2 is perhaps critical, but then Black has 9...c5. This made Nakamura play 9.♘bd2, but he was soon strategically worse.

7...♘a6

The logical move, and what Tiviakov recommends, even though the computer insists that after 7...b5 8.♕b3 ♕c8 9.♕xb5 c6 Black has very decent compensation for the sacrificed pawn.

8.♘c3 ♘c5

White has managed to block the b7-bishop, but in this manner Black again gets ready for ...♘fe4.

9.♘d4

The straightforward move, and while it to some extent plays into Black's hand, it is in no way bad. More solid moves exist, e.g. 9.♕c2, but once again, Erigaisi is afraid of nobody.

9...e5!

An integral party of Tiviakov's concept. It may look as if Black is aiming for a Queen's Indian, but then changes his mind and goes for a King's Indian instead. Meanwhile, White has been making useful and logical moves. However, the small details are somewhat in Black's favour. For a start, White is losing some time moving his knight around the board, and secondly, although grabbing space in the centre with d5

is very typical in the King's Indian, one could argue that, while it does indeed block the black b7-bishop, the same can be said of White's bishop at g2. Again, we are not at all talking of Black being better, but an unusual structure has arisen in which Black is not really worse.

10.♘c2

After 10.♘b3 d6 11.♘xc5 Tiviakov played the interesting 11...dxc5!?, rerouting the knight to d6. Erigaisi's choice is logical. Since he has more space, he avoids exchanges.

10...a5 11.b3 d6 12.e4 ♗c8!

With the structure has dramatically changed, this back-and-forth is fully justified. The bishop now supports ...f5, and the b7-square, perhaps surprisingly, is very useful for the black knight in terms of blockading the queenside structure, as we will see later.

13.♘a3 ♘e8 14.♘ab5 ♗d7

15.♖b1?!

15.a3 was the better move order, since the computer then wants to meet 15...f5 with 16.exf5, when having the rook on b1 allows ...♗xf5!? The concept is that after 16...gxf5 17.♖b1 Black's

attack on the kingside is less easy to develop than in the game.

15...f5 16.f3 f4 17.a3

17...g5

A noteworthy choice. At some stage in the evolution of King's Indian understanding, Black started to avoid playing this, since it blocks his dark-squared bishop, as it does here. 17...h5!? was a way to progress without allowing White to play the immediate g4, but the computers are not particularly impressed. In sharp contrast, they point to 17...a4!, the idea being that 18.b4 ♘b3 allows Black to take the bishop on c1, followed by ...♗h6, and if 18.♘xa4 then 18...♘xa4 19.bxa4 ♗h6!? 20.g4 ♗g5!. One can see the aforementioned black concept in action, with the black-squared bishop being active on h4, even though the computers say that 21.♔f2!? ♗h4+ 22.♔e2 is a decent counter-thrust, evacuating the white king towards the centre!

18.b4 ♘b7

As mentioned above, this is a clever square for the knight, controlling White's potential c5 break, as well as keeping an eye on a5.

19.g4 h5 20.h3

It is fair to say that the position is closed, but not yet fully static. At first sight, it seems as if only Black has a pawn break, with the potential ...c6, but King's Indian knowledge tells us that Black may aim at sacrificing on g4, while White may consider pushing c5, even as a pawn sacrifice. Obviously, this means that while the players try to carry out their own plan, they simultaneously try and prevent their opponent's plan from being executed.

20...♖f7 21.♔f2! ♗f8 22.♖g1 ♖h7 23.♗f1 ♘f6 24.♔e1 ♕c8 25.♖b2 ♘d8

In his new book *Rock Solid Chess*, Sergey Tiviakov describes the virtues of the double fianchetto so well that Magnus Carlsen decided to try it in his last-round game against Arjun Erigaisi.

26.♕d3?!
Magnus has managed a 'changing of the guard' against the c5-break and now starts transferring his knight, so that it will be able to join the breakthrough attempt on the kingside. However, while the price of being inaccurate has not been high during the last few moves, here is an exception. The computer now indicates 26...axb4! as strong, as after 27.axb4 hxg4 28.hxg4 c6! Black exploits the opportunity to catch his opponent off-guard. The main point is that after 29.dxc6 ♘xc6, Black threatens 30...d5, attacking b4, and if 30.♘xd6 then 30...♘xb4 31.♖xb4 ♕c5! wins.
26...♘f7?! 27.♔d1 ♗e7 28.♔c2 axb4?!
A winning inaccuracy? That's way too strong a statement. Yet, while the computer is not impressed by Magnus's move, it makes sense from a practical perspective, since staying put would make it difficult to make

progress. And since Wijk aan Zee is one of the few tournaments in which the players get an extra hour after move 40, it was a good idea to intensify the struggle while both players were relatively short on time.

29.axb4 hxg4 30.hxg4 ♖a1 31.♖b1 ♖h2+ 32.♖g2?!
A tempting move. Why not go for exchanges? But this is precisely what helps Black. Better was 32.♗e2. It is understandable that Erigaisi wanted to exchange rooks, as Black's rook on h2 is more active, but keeping g4 firmly protected was a bigger priority. And with the a-file opened, Black would also be taking a risk, as the white rook could suddenly become active there!

32...♖xg2+ 33.♗xg2 ♖xb1 34.♔xb1

34...♘xg4!
A good move, and a logical one for the flow of the game. The computer gives its usual 0.00 verdict, yet the practical chances are now with Black.
35.fxg4 ♗xg4 36.♗f3!?
There was no immediate hurry. Black's threat is to prepare pushing his pawns on the kingside, and for that he had to withdraw his bishop from g4 anyway. However, Erigaisi sees this as an opportunity to transfer his bishop to h5, where it eyes the black king and knight, while also keeping an eye on the black pawns in case they start marching forward, but from a more forward outpost.

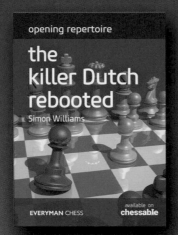
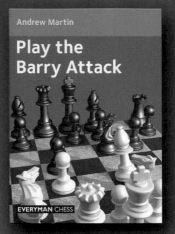

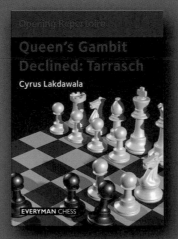
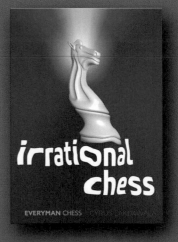

36...♗h3 37.♗h5 g4 38.♘e2 ♗f1!?

Magnus also uses the whole board, and the bishop forces the white queen to retreat.

39.♕d1 ♗g2 40.♗g6 ♘g5

A fascinating position, unless you are a computer, which just keeps repeating 0.00. Magnus tries to gain time by attacking e4, and while Erigaisi had played optimistically thus far, he now falls back into passivity. 41.♘xf4!? was possible, as after 41...exf4 42.♗b2 it is suddenly White who starts attacking, and the long diagonal is vulnerable. Still 0.00, though!

41.♘bc3?! ♗f3 42.♕f1? ♔g7!

While it may look at first sight as if Black's plan is ...g3, Magnus had a much stronger concept in mind. He has cleared the eighth rank for his queen to access the h3-square via h8. As White cannot exchange on h3, because this would allow the black pawn to queen, this means that Black penetrates on the kingside. The computers already give the verdict: Black is winning.

43.♗f5 ♕h8 44.♘xf4

Desperation, but understandable. Just sitting passively left zero chances.

44...exf4 45.♗xf4 ♗f6 46.♕c1 ♘f7! The piece has been won back, and Black switches to solidity again, removing the knight from White's threat and aiming for the e5-square.

47.♘b5 ♕a8 48.e5?!

48.♕a3 was the absolutely last chance, even though the endgame is obviously much better for Black.

48...dxe5 49.♗d2 ♘d6!

Allowing some checks, but they only improve Black's position.

50.♗h6+ ♔f7 51.♘xd6+ cxd6 52.♗g5 ♕h8!

The last key move to control the h6-square and stop the white queen

from entering. With no counterplay left, White's position is hopeless.

53.♗e3 e4 54.♗xb6 ♕h2 55.♗g1 ♕e2! 56.b5 ♕d3+

And with both 57.♕c2 ♕a3 and 57.♔a2 ♗d1 leading to immediate mate, Erigaisi resigned.

■ ■ ■

Impressive, for sure, but it wasn't enough. And Carlsen knew it when Erigaisi resigned, as meanwhile, Giri had won his game against Richard Rapport.

NOTES BY
Anish Giri

Anish Giri
Richard Rapport
Wijk aan Zee Masters 2023 (13)
Sicilian Defence, Richter-Rauzer Variation

1.e4 c5 2.♘f3 d6 I recalled Richard Rapport playing a bunch of different openings, but I must admit that the Sicilian he was about to play was not at the top of my list.

3.d4 cxd4 4.♘xd4 ♘f6 5.♘c3 ♘c6 The Classical Sicilian wasn't too unexpected, because Richard had played it at the Candidates tournament in Madrid last summer, in the final round against Nepo, the eventual winner.

6.♗g5 g6!?

But this was a surprise. I had seen this passing by, not least thanks to the efforts of Daniil Dubov, who plays this line a lot, though I guess mainly in games with a faster time-control. I have also encountered it multiple times in my lichess bullet practice, and after continuously getting into trouble with White, I eventually found a practical bullet antidote.

7.♗xf6 exf6 8.♗b5!?
I spent quite some time thinking about whether I was seriously going to play my bullet opening in this very crucial game, instead of trying to recollect the actual theory and win the d6-pawn. After quite some thought, I decided that yes, I was going to.
8.♗c4 ♗g7 9.♘db5 0-0 10.♕xd6 is the old main line, which is pretty much what Black is hoping for, with the ...f5 break looming.

8...♗d7 9.♗c4!? ♗g7 10.♘xc6
The point of the previous move. Now Black has to capture with the bishop, since the bishop is no longer hanging on b5 after ...bxc6, and White can just collect the d6-pawn.

10...♗xc6

Without the knights the position is much less exciting. White has control of the d5-square, in Sveshnikov Variation style, whereas Black isn't going

After a poor first half, Richard Rapport suddenly won three games, but the Romanian left Wijk aan Zee after a last-round loss against tournament winner Anish Giri.

to get much fun going, even after the thematic ...f5 break.

11.0-0 0-0 12.♕d3
It seemed more sensible to start with ♕d3, rather than ♘d5, which would allow queenside expansion with ...b5.

12...♖c8 Now ...f5 becomes more of a realistic idea, due to the pressure along the c-file.

13.♘d5 I was very happy with my knight here.

13...♖e8 14.c3

For a second I thought the position looked too good to be true, but Richard's strong next move reminded me that it couldn't be this easy.

14...♗d7! A strong rerouting move. I didn't see much point to it, since I saw I could meet it with 15.♗b5, but upon closer inspection I realized that

15...♗c6 back is stronger than it looks, as it contains the positional 'threat' of ...♗xd5! (when ♗xe8? runs into ...♗c4!).

15.♗b5

15...♗c6!
As said, Black wants to take on d5, which isn't immediately obvious, but has to do with the fact that it's crucial for White to control the d5-square with the bishop. After considering all the options, I realized I didn't see even the slightest hint of an edge here and that I would have to look again after 16.♗c4 ♗d7.

16.♗c4 ♗d7
The deeper I delved into the position, the more I realized that I had been too happy with myself, and that all I had

was a pretty much equal position that was just a tad easier to play.

17.♖fe1!

Not a thrilling idea, to just allow ...f5, but in fact this is the best White has. In the resulting positions it is still slightly easier to play with White, thanks to the pretty knight on d5 and a somewhat weak d6-pawn.

17.♘e3 was another idea I considered, but the problem is the 17...♗h6! resource, right away or after 17...♗c6 18.♗d5.

17...f5 In fact, the engine suggests delaying this push with 17...♖c5, and after 18.♗b3 to start with 18...a5!?, but I was also expecting the immediate ...f5.

18.♗b3 The simplest moves are often the best. **18...fxe4 19.♖xe4**

19...♗f5 20.♖xe8+ ♕xe8 21.♕d2 ♗e6 Richard was playing pretty solidly here, but my position now felt ever so slightly better.

22.♖d1 This is more clever than the superficial move ♖e1. Nothing is happening on the e-file, while some potential pressure on the d6-pawn might be a factor.

22...♕d7 23.h3

Maybe ♘e3 first was a tad more accurate, but I wanted to give my king some luft, before deciding what to do next. Also, I was considering queen moves like ♕f4-g5 or ♕e3.

23...b5 24.♕f4 ♖c5 25.♘e3!

25...♗e5?! A natural move, but the bishop is in the way here apparently, while it kicks the queen to an even better square.

A much more harmonious way to guard the d6-pawn was 25...♖e5!, but to be frank I didn't quite understand what Black would have to do exactly either. I just felt that things were starting to go well for me.

26.♕e4 ♔g7

27.f4

I felt it was time for action and decided to override my instincts and push pawns, upping the heat.

The computer points out a much more elegant and efficient way to do things: 27.♘xe6!. Unfortunately, since I hadn't seen a forced win, I was rather dismissive of this capture, since I didn't want Black to regain control of the crucial d5-square. However, it works due to some concrete factors: 27...fxe6 28.♘g4!.

ANALYSIS DIAGRAM

A nasty resource. The knight turns out to be really good here, pressuring the e5-bishop: 28...♕c7 29.♕e3. With f4 being a threat, 29...♗f7 is the only move, which isn't too harmonious. The computer also likes 29.♔f1!, which is even more sophisticated, preparing for some concrete variations after ♘xe5 ♖xe5 ♕d4, when the back rank might matter.

27...♗f6 28.g4

It was not the time to hesitate. Besides just advancing the pawn for psychological effect, the move also has a very concrete point. I now have the threat of 29.♗xe6 fxe6 29.g5 ♗e7 30.♕d4+, followed by ♕xc5.

28...h6 I hadn't expected this move and almost blitzed out a reply that I had prepared for 28...♔g8, which actually was the best move there.

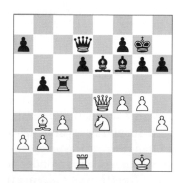

29.♗d5?!

Missing a very neat tactical motif: 29.♗xe6! fxe6 30.h4!, renewing the threat of 31. g5 ♕d4+ 32. ♕xc5. Black is in quite some trouble here and has to try and survive with 30...♗f7!, when after h5, ♕h7+ and g5 he will face a dangerous attack.

29...♗xd5!

Richard makes use of the opportunity and sets up timely counterplay.
30.♘xd5 ♖c4!

I had underestimated Black activating the rook via the 4th rank, but now I just had to go with the flow.
31.♕f3 ♕e6 Black is getting all his pieces to work together again.
32.f5!? As ...♗h4 and ...♖e4 were all coming, the only way at this point was to go forward.
32...gxf5 33.♘f4!? The other option, 33.♘e3, which I initially liked, got dismissed due to 33...fxg4 34.hxg4 ♕e4!?, which annoyed me greatly, so I switched to this idea.

33...♕e5 I was actually recalling Richard surviving a game against Ding Liren when he was an exchange down, which made me wonder how bad 33...♖xf4!? was, when after 34.♕xf4 ♕xa2 Black looks OK. However, this time he didn't want to part with his rook. There was no need for it either. In fact, at this point Black already has some options, since even 34...♕e7!? is apparently a good move as well. The thing is that even though White may get solid control of the f5-square, the king is too

weakened to expect to get much from this position.
34.♘h5+
Now 34...♔g6?? would obviously lose to 35.♖xd6, so I was focused on ...♔h7 and ...♔g8/♔h8. After 34...♔h7, 35.♖f1 looked promising, and after 34...♔g8 / ♔h8 I suddenly saw a fascinating variation with 35.♕a8+ ♔h7 36.♕e8!! ♖c7(??) 37.♖d5!. Excited about the resource that had just occurred to me and before I could continue to calculate these lines, Richard suddenly made his move.

34...♔g6??
It was quite shocking to see this happen, because the next cheapo was the entire point of the sequence that I had played so far and I would never have expected this to happen, let alone at such a crucial moment.
After 34...♔h7 35.♖f1 b4 Black is OK, since he gets enough counterplay.
And after 34...♔g8, 35.♕a8+ is neither better nor worse than other moves (the natural 35.♖f1 would be the alternative, with dynamic equality, even though White's position may seem more threatening at this point) 35...♔h7 36.♕e8

ANALYSIS DIAGRAM

36...♗g7!. This was the simple resource that I hadn't seen.
Also possible is to start with 36...fxg4 37.♕xf7+ ♔g7, when White should stop trying and just simplify into a draw. 36...♖c7? 37.♖d5!! is indeed picturesque.

35.♖xd6!
I spent quite some time verifying that I wouldn't blunder anything, because that is the luxury one can afford in classical chess, and also because of the importance of this moment. I noticed 35...♔g5!?, but then, after spotting 36.♖d5!, I knew this should all be over.
35...♔g5 36.♖d5!
This is the clinical way. It's over now.
36...♕e1+ 37.♔g2 ♗e7

The rest is easy and of course, instead of trying to find a checkmate, I just traded queens, even further improving on the saying that it's better to win a queen than to go for a checkmate, because the checkmate can suddenly not be there.
38.♖xf5+ ♔h4 39.♕g3+
Black will get mated in the endgame anyway, so Richard resigned.
At this point, Jorden's position also clarified and it had become quite clear that this victory was going to be special.

■ ■ ■

Having won his game, Anish Giri was on the brink of his first win in the Tata Steel Masters, as Abdusattorov, despite the white pieces, was in deep trouble against Van Foreest. Would his compatriot convert his advantage or would he let the leader off the hook with a draw? A draw was certainly the last thing Giri wanted, since it would mean a blitz tiebreak match for the title with the Uzbek youngster – a terrifying thought with the traumatic tie-break losses against Carlsen in

Giri even went so far as to say he might not play the tie-breaker

2018 and against Van Foreest in 2021 etched in his mind. Giri even went so far as to say he might not play the tie-breaker, as it did not make any sense in his eyes. This was clearly nervousness, and seeing there was no way he could refuse to play a tie-break, he announced that he would play only because his oldest son wanted to see him play and he had arrived too late with the rest of his family to watch his game against Rapport.

In the end, there was no need to be nervous, as Van Foreest decided the outcome of the Tata Steel Masters by inflicting Abdusattorov's first and only defeat.

NOTES BY
Jorden van Foreest

Nodirbek Abdusattorov
Jorden van Foreest
Wijk aan Zee Masters 2023 (13)
Sicilian Defence, Taimanov Variation

1.e4 c5 I had been looking forward to this game. Abdusattorov had been playing a stellar tournament and

could win the tournament outright by beating me. On the other hand, I had been playing fairly well in the last five games, picking up some confidence along the way. Although I did not necessarily mind a draw as Black going into this game versus the tournament leader, I did not want to play supersolidly either. I decided to give the Sicilian a try and see how it would go.

2.♘f3 e6 3.d4
I had thought that Abdusattorov might play the Alapin (2.c3) for solidity, since a draw would guarantee him at least a play-off, but it seems that my opponent did not mind a fully-fletched battle either.

3...cxd4 4.♘xd4 ♘c6 5.♘c3 ♕c7

My choice had fallen upon the Taimanov, which used to be my main repertoire when I was still looking for big fights as Black on a regular basis.

6.♗e3 a6 7.♕f3
I remember when this idea appeared on the scene. It was around 2014, and it looked very strange to me. Now we have moved on almost 10 years, and this could actually be regarded as the modern main line of the Taimanov. In many lines, White wants to play ♕g3, acquiring a slightly better endgame.

7...h5 There is also the variation 7...♘e5 8.♕g3 h5, but as it turns out, Black can also do without the knight move first.

8.0-0-0 In case of 8.♕g3, there is the option 8...d6, avoiding the queen swap.

8...b5 9.♕g3 ♕xg3 Black is forced to trade queens in this scenario, as 9...d6 runs into the crushing 10.♗xb5 axb5 11.♘dxb5, followed by 12.♘xd6, a typical sacrifice in the Sicilian.

10.hxg3 ♗c5

An important move, as Black typically does not mind exchanging a couple of pieces. The pressure on the d4-knight is also slightly awkward for White.

11.g4 The most direct move, but not necessarily the best.

11...♗b7
Although I was not familiar with this exact position, I was aware of the idea of giving up the h5-pawn in order to achieve quick development.

12.f3
After 12.♖xh5 ♖xh5 13.gxh5 ♘f6 14.♗e2 ♖c8. Black's active pieces provide sufficient resources to compensate for the loss of the pawn. The main idea here is ...♘xd4, followed by ...♘xe4, which is surprisingly hard to stop, since the natural 15.f3 leaves the h5-pawn unprotected.

12...g6?!
An alternative worth considering was 12...h4, which would have amplified Black's control over the dark squares. Although I had some concerns about White's 13.g3 during the game, Black's 13...g5 response keeps everything adequately defendable.

13.♘f5

The choice to swap bishops was a logical one, as it reduces the pressure along the a7-g1 diagonal.

13...♗xe3+ 14.♘xe3 ♚e7

The handshake at the start of their game left no doubt that both Nodirbek Abdusattorov and Jorden van Foreest were looking for a big fight on the last day.

I quite liked my centralized king here, protecting the dark squares. Interestingly, the engine recommends 14...0-0-0, which somehow feels less natural to me, but does immediately allow the rook into the game.

15.♗e2 d6

Black would prefer to play 15...♘f6, but this move is hindered by White's 16.g5, pushing the knight to an uncomfortable square. The current move clears the d7-square, paving the way for an eventual ...♘f6.

16.g5

I had anticipated my opponent to at long last capture the h5-pawn, as it grants White a modest yet enduring advantage, particularly given the tournament standings.

16...f6 17.f4!?

This move, however, caught me off guard. I was confident that he would capture the f6-pawn, which appeared to leave the position roughly balanced.

The text opts for a bold approach, but it also entails considerable strategic risks, as White sacrifices his pawn structure and cedes control of the desirable e5-square. As a result, White's play will now hinge entirely on keeping the g8-knight out of the game.

17...fxg5 18.fxg5 ♘e5 19.♖d4

19...♖d8? A grave error, presenting White with a chance to gain a significant advantage.

19...♘c6 would have been better, but the point is very subtle, and not at all easy to spot over the board: 20.♖d2 ♘e5 21.♖hd1 ♖d8. White's only plan here is to play for a4, but with the rook on d2, this won't work that well, since ...b4 is a convenient reply. Therefore, White's best bet appears to be to repeat moves with 22.♖d4 ♘c6 23.♖4d2, etc.

20.♖hd1?! Failing to seize the opportunity. After 20.a4 ♘c6 21.♖d2 b4 22.♘cd1 Black's queenside is severely compromised, and the d1-knight can re-enter the game via the f2-square, granting White a sizable advantage.

20...h4?! Allowing White a second chance. It was not too late to transpose to the variation above with 20...♘c6 21.♖4d2 ♘e5, etc.

21.♘g4

After lengthy deliberation, Abdusattorov once again spares me. It appears that he had a fascinating plan in mind, which upon initial examination appears to be highly alluring.

21...♘c6 22.♖4d2 ♖h5

Although I was sure that my opponent had something up his sleeve against this logical plan of simply capturing the g5-pawn, I did not see it and decided to just go for it.

‘It was only here that the full extent of Abdusattorov’s plan dawned on me. Unfortunately, at this point, there was no turning back’

23.e5 It was only here that the full extent of Abdusattorov’s plan dawned on me. Unfortunately, at this point, there was no turning back. Suddenly, however, I also spotted an intriguing response to my opponent’s idea...
23...d5 24.♘e4!

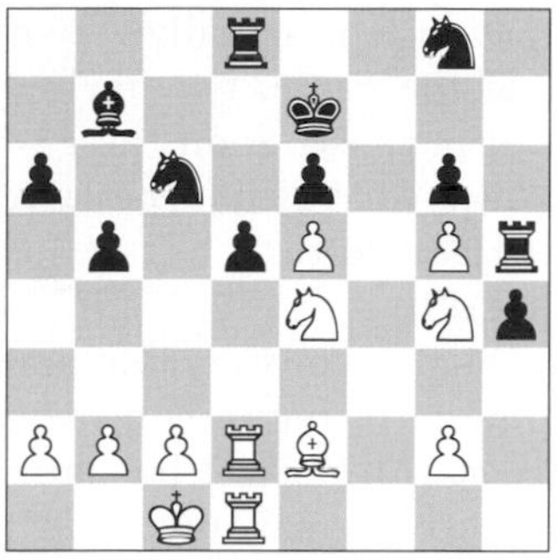

A fantastic idea. White suddenly sacrifices a full knight!
24...♗c8
It was this reply that I had spotted the move before. As it turns out, White has no actual threats in the position and this simple retreat of the bishop is highly unpleasant to meet. White’s problem is that if he cannot find an immediate way to find play, both the g5- and e5-pawns will be sitting ducks, and are likely to fall prey to Black’s pieces sooner or later.
After 24...dxe4 25.♖xd8 ♘xd8, 26.♘f6 seems absolutely crushing, but amazingly this is still alright for Black, too: 26...♖xg5 27.♖d7+ ♔f8 28.♖xd8+ ♔f7.

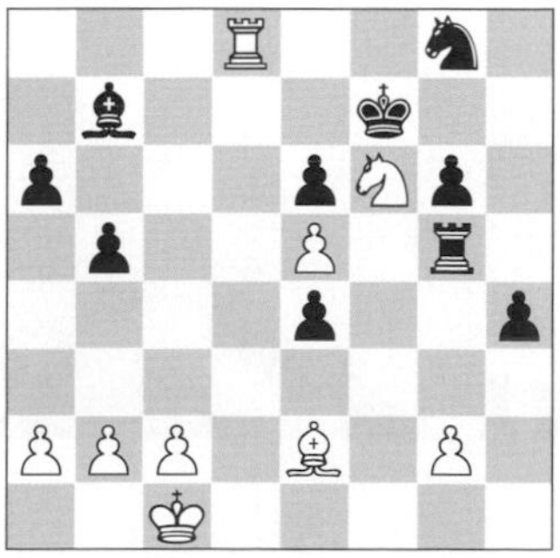

ANALYSIS DIAGRAM

White can capture either the knight on g8, or the bishop on b7 with ♖d7+, but in all cases Black will reply with ...♖xg2, upon which the advanced h-pawn will provide enough counterplay for a draw.
25.♘gf6? The most logical reply, but actually a serious mistake.
25.♘gf2! would have kept the game objectively roughly equal, but humanly this backward knight move is hard to consider: after 25...♖h8 26.♘d6 ♘xe5 27.♘xc8+ ♖xc8 28.♖e1, although Black has won a pawn, the knight on g8 is still very much out of the game, and the king on e7 is slightly unsafe as well.
25...♖h8

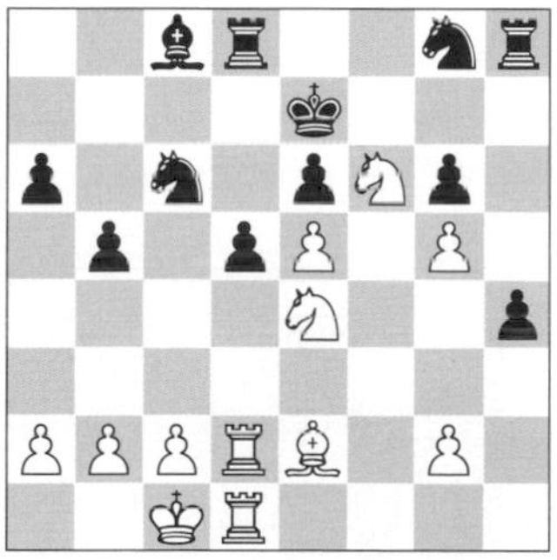

26.♘xg8+?! Perhaps better chances were offered by 26.a4, looking to disturb Black on the queenside, but once again, this is hard to understand from a human point of view, as there is no clear follow-up after 26...bxa4, and only computers manage to come up with obscure ways to find counterplay.
26...♖dxg8 27.♘f6 ♖d8 28.♖e1

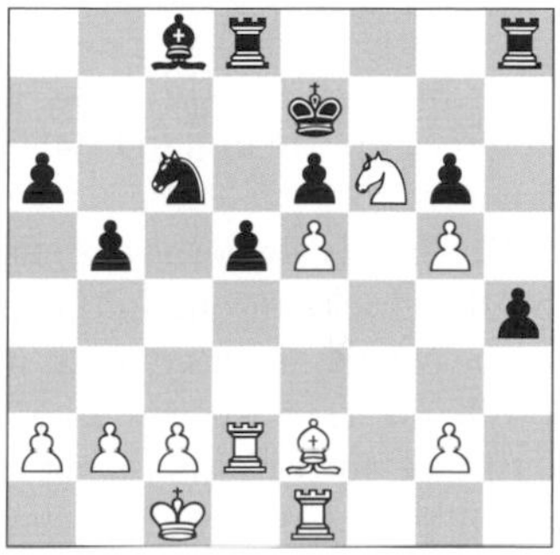

28...h3? Missing a serious chance. After 28...♘xe5 29.♗xb5 I stopped my calculations, but I should have looked one move further: 29...h3!. The bone-crusher! All the tactics work out in Black’s favour here, the main point being that 30.gxh3 is met by 30...♘f3, forking White’s rooks.
29.gxh3 ♖xh3 30.♗g4?
A strange move, as the bishop has no future here. It would have been better,

Wijk aan Zee Masters 2023

				1	2	3	4	5	6	7	8	9	10	11	12	13	14		TPR
1	Anish Giri	IGM 2764	NED	*	½	1	½	½	½	½	1	½	½	1	1	½	½	8½	2849
2	Nodirbek Abdusattorov	IGM 2713	UZB	½	*	1	½	1	½	½	1	0	½	½	½	½	1	8	2830
3	Magnus Carlsen	IGM 2859	NOR	0	0	*	½	1	1	½	1	½	½	½	½	1	1	8	2819
4	Wesley So	IGM 2760	USA	½	½	½	*	½	½	½	½	½	½	1	½	1	½	7½	2797
5	Parham Maghsoodloo	IGM 2719	IRI	½	0	0	½	*	½	1	½	1	1	0	½	½	1	7	2772
6	Fabiano Caruana	IGM 2766	USA	½	½	0	½	½	*	½	½	1	½	1	½	½	½	7	2768
7	Levon Aronian	IGM 2735	USA	½	½	½	½	0	½	*	½	½	½	½	½	1	½	6½	2742
8	Richard Rapport	IGM 2740	ROU	0	0	0	½	½	½	½	*	½	1	½	1	½	1	6½	2741
9	Jorden van Foreest	IGM 2681	NED	½	1	½	½	0	0	½	½	*	0	½	½	½	1	6	2717
10	R Praggnanandhaa	IGM 2684	IND	½	½	½	½	0	½	½	0	1	*	0	1	½	½	6	2716
11	Gukesh D	IGM 2725	IND	0	½	½	0	1	0	½	½	½	1	*	0	½	½	5½	2685
12	Ding Liren	IGM 2811	CHN	0	½	½	½	½	½	½	0	½	0	1	*	½	½	5½	2679
13	Vincent Keymer	IGM 2696	GER	½	½	0	0	½	½	0	½	½	½	½	½	*	½	5	2658
14	Arjun Erigaisi	IGM 2722	IND	½	0	0	½	0	½	½	0	0	½	½	½	½	*	4	2602

and more logical to play 30.♗d3 instead, keeping an eye on the g6-pawn. **30...♖h4 31.b3 ♖dh8**

Only at this point did I feel that I should really be on top, so I started to play for a win.

32.♔b2 Already we both were slightly low on the clock, and had no time to assess the consequences of each move. Although the text is very logical, it allows Black to initiate a rook swap, which will diminish any white chances of counterplay.

The pawn sacrifice 32.c4, intending to open the position, would still have provided White with a decent amount of counterplay: 32...dxc4 33.bxc4 bxc4 34.♗f3! (now the c6-knight is being disturbed) 34...♘b4 35.♗e4, and the bishop has successfully rerouted itself to a better square, and White is active enough to maintain the balance.

32...♖h2 33.♖ee2 ♖xe2 34.♖xe2 a5

Gaining some space on the queenside.

35.a3 ♗a6 36.♖e1 b4

37.a4?

In my opinion, this was a crucial error, as it effectively stripped White of all counterplay. The only good reply was 37.axb4, still giving White some play along the open a-file.

Note how White is virtually unable to move any of his pieces, and the knight on f6 is actually very much out of the game, not having any useful purpose. Soon the g5- and e5-pawns will be ripe to be harvested by the black forces.

37...♘d8

I devoted a considerable amount of time to trying to win the game outright with 37...♖h2, but ultimately I was unable to make this work. In the end, I opted for a simpler approach, focusing on capturing White's pawns without delay.

After 37...♖h2 38.♘g8+ ♔f7 39.♘h6+ ♔g7 40.♗xe6 I could not find a win, but as it turns out, there actually was one: 40...♘d4 41.♗xd5 ♖xc2+

(41...♘xc2 42.♖h1! was a saving resource I spotted) 42.♔b1.

ANALYSIS DIAGRAM

Here 42...♖c5! is the winning blow (I mostly looked at 42...♗d3, but stunningly enough, there is no win after 43.♖d1), which I had missed. ...♗d3+ will follow, and White is completely helpless.

38.♗e2
Capitulation, but already it was hard to offer any good advice.

38...♗xe2 39.♖xe2 ♘f7 40.c3

A desperate attempt, but without any pawns, White will lose soon.

40...bxc3+ 41.♔xc3 ♘xg5 42.b4 ♖h3+ 43.♔b2 axb4 44.♖c2 ♘f3

The cleanest solution. White has no

After five second places, the trophy was finally his. No matter how rational Anish Giri's reaction and analysis was, it was also clear that the Dutchman was very happy with his victory.

more than a few checks, and in due course, Black will capture the e5- and a4-pawns.

45.♘g4 ♘d4 46.♖c8 ♖b3+ 47.♔a2 ♖a3+ 48.♔b2 ♖xa4 49.♘f6 b3 White resigned and the tournament came to a thrilling conclusion for me. Although this was a bitter disappointment for Abdusattorov, who had displayed exceptional chess skills throughout, it secured Anish's first victory in Wijk aan Zee.

■ ■ ■

Giri's victory was celebrated as a combined Dutch feat, which only added to the festive mood. As Giri put it – not missing a chance to include witty references to Rapport's recent transfer to the Romanian federation and earlier transfers to the USCF – 'During the games, it felt at some point (as if) I was playing a team match. It reminded me of the Olympiad, when me and Jorden had to beat the other team, some strange team that decided to buy Richard and Nodirbek – could

be USA in a couple of years, who knows!'

In a first reaction, Magnus Carlsen said he felt bad for Nodirbek Abdusattorov, who had been leading all through the tournament, but that he also had 'huge congrats' for Anish Giri. 'He broke a lot of records. He won a super-tournament, he beat me for the first time in a long time. (...) He's been very close so many times. I guess he was somewhat fortunate today, but on the other hand, looking at the games he had and the positions he had through the tournament, his win is not remotely undeserved.'

Abdusattorov looked back on his performance with admirable composure and maturity: 'I was very disappointed after the last round, but after all it was my first super-tournament. I hadn't enough experience, so I see a lot of bright sides to this tournament. I fully accept my result.'

And Anish Giri? He will tell you more in the interview in this issue. Not to be missed! ■

Fair & Square

Yevgeny Prigozhin: 'The strategy of Wagner PMC is a chess game, where there is another chess game inside the course of each piece. For those who do not play chess, I will explain. This is not a game in which you need to hit the head with a chessboard, so that the opponent shouts: "Uhi, Uhi, Uchi!"' *(The head of private Russian military group Wagner on February 4, responding to a question about rumours of a new Russian offensive in Ukraine)*

Mikhail Tal: 'The future of chess is in no danger, though the abundance of information can cloud your head. Sadly, young players pay too much attention to this "factological" side of chess *(variations, variations)*. But I still believe in fantasy.' *(Said during a televised lecture in 1988)*

Joey Votto: 'I think the soup I had for lunch helped carry me to my first chess win. Or was it the barley.' *(The six-time MLB All-Star's Instagram post as he returned to Toronto's Annex Chess Club for a second tournament in late January, scoring his first competitive OTB win. We suggest he next try the soup experience in Wijk aan Zee!)*

Arthur Bisguier: 'Zugzwang is like getting trapped on a safety island in the middle of a highway when a thunderstorm starts.'

Fabiano Caruana: 'Classical chess is dying a slow death.' *(Speaking after the Tata Steel Masters about the huge effort to prepare and play in a major tournament, when he can earn twice as much online in the Champions Chess Tour without having to leave his home)*

Tony Miles: 'A cable.' *(The legendary telegram sent to his national federation, after an official asked him to send a cable in 1976 from Dubna, Russia, should he gain his final norm to become Britain's first Grandmaster)*

Humpy Koneru: 'I now have an aspect of my life that's untouched by how well or how badly I play. That helps put even my worst results into perspective. The day I drop sharply in the rankings and don't have the results to show for the time I spend away from Ahana, I'll stop playing.' *(In the January 15 feature article for The Sunday Hindustan Times, on how the Indian No 1 woman player's family life, following the birth of her daughter, has balanced her life)*

Olimpiu Di Luppi (b. Urcan): 'Internet chess is a black hole that consumes people's souls piece by piece.' *(Tweeted by the Singapore-based chess historian and writer)*

Peter Svidler: 'The biggest tool for chess improvement would be playing against stronger opposition.' *(Words of wisdom from the Chess24 commentator to chess fans looking to improve their game during the recent Airthings Masters)*

Jan Gustafsson: 'It's just no fun to play chess – so many questions!' *(The Chess24 commentator during the recent Airthings Masters)*

Carlos Torre Repetto: 'I have the impression that he played with a view to the endgame. He saw, or felt, what had to be done in any position.' *(The Mexican enigma writing in the mid-1920s on world champion Jose Raul Capablanca)*

Ding Liren: 'You have to prepare mentally, you have to imagine what will happen if you are in the centre of people and there will be only one game, and every eye will watch you.' *(On preparing for his World Championship match with Ian Nepomniachtchi in April)*

Juan José Arreola: 'I play chess and sometimes I abuse it, because instead of one or two games I play six or seven, and when I was younger I played more. The first thing I can tell you is that I don't feel tired even if I have played a lot, but if I lose, I am annihilated, exhausted. So the feeling of winning in chess is one of the best affirmations of one's personality.' *(The Mexican writer and humorist, interviewed in the October 1997 edition of Ajedrez de Mexico on his passion for the game)*

When they were young

The trend of top grandmasters becoming younger and younger has been clearly visible in Wijk aan Zee. In 1985, the average age of the participants in the top group was 33. Twenty years later the average age had slightly dropped to 30 years. The 2023 edition of the Tata Steel Masters saw an average age of 25. That means that most of the boys in the pictures below (all born in 1990 or later) would have been considered fairly old there! What are their names?

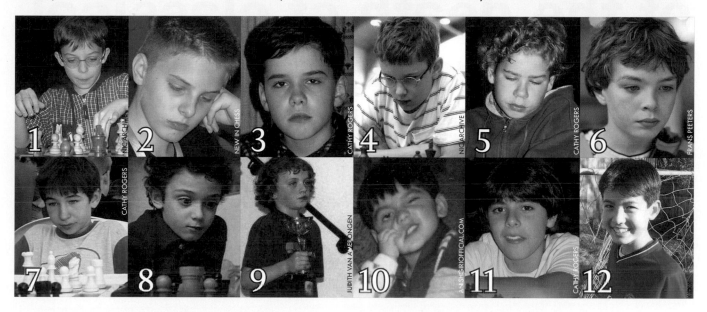

If you fill in their names below you will see that the letters in the numbered spaces will produce a word (to be filled in underneath). That word is the solution to this quiz that was taken from Dimitri Reinderman's *The Chess Pub Quiz Puzzle Book* (New In Chess 2023).

#																				
1	5			4	5			1		3	4		14				14			
2	14				6	14		14	6			14								
3		7	7				10		11			13			13	11				
4	15			14		8	12						9		15					
5		7		9				3		5	5		14							
6	14			7		1	7		14			12								
7	5	4			8	6			4		4	7								
8	15	2				15				15										
9	13		12	7			10		7		10	1				3				11
11	6		8	6		6		4		12		15		11		13				

Solution:

1	2	3	4	5	6	7	8	9	10	11	12	13	14	15

The names of the players and the word that is the solution to this quiz you can find on page 104.

Anish Giri:

'It seems the rumours of the death of classical chess are somewhat exaggerated'

Winning the Tata Steel Masters was the dream start of what he sees as 'a big year'. In an extensive interview, Anish Giri reveals his ambitions and expectations, speaking freely about his current focus on classical chess, Magnus Carlsen (of course), swapping seconds and the evolution and future of our game.

by JONATHAN TISDALL

Anish Giri's victory in the Tata Steel Masters after a dramatic last-round finish attracted a lot of media attention, both in the Netherlands and in the worldwide chess community. Amid the euphoria and excitement, the winner himself remained remarkably sober and down-to-earth. Questions about his plans to celebrate were invariably answered with an apologetic smile and the explanation that he is not the partying type. Yes, he was happy, but not ecstatic.

Together with his wife Sopiko and his young sons Daniel and Michael, the tournament winner attended the traditional pea soup dinner and the prize-giving, where his parents and sisters were also present. Later in the evening he left the hotel where he had been staying for more than two weeks and drove home to The Hague. He knew the days ahead were going to be packed, including an appearance in a major television talk show, and was in deadly serious mode. Following his win, we had talked only briefly in Wijk aan Zee, but he agreed on an extensive interview via Skype and we duly found a slot at the end of the week.

Our first conversation, an interview after Giri's victory in the 2021 Magnus Carlsen Invitational, had been planned to be short but gone on for hours – even though he had been in the midst of preparation for the Candidates – so there was a sense of mutual concern not to let Anish overdo it again.

There was only a mild moment of panic when Anish didn't pick up his virtual videophone, but he messaged to say that this was just due to a brief clash with his tea-making. A minute later, we were connected, the Tata champion looking serene in a speckled blue hoodie, and sure enough, with a steaming mug by his side.

To start on light topics: Can you rank three things for me on a scale of 1-10? Winning your first Tata...
'A scale of what – joy?'

Yes, call it joy – happiness...
'You have to leave a number for winning the Candidates or becoming World Champion, so I'll call it an 8.'

Beating Magnus again?
'On the same scale, I guess a 7.'

Anish Giri on Magnus Carlsen's dominance in classical chess: 'If you are fed up and uninterested and you've got all these great talented youngsters who are super eager and also super good, it is not a given that he will stay number one forever.'

LENNART OOTES

The game against Gukesh? Please tell me that wasn't all prep. Whenever I am impressed with something nowadays someone tells me that it was all prep.

'No, no. ...♔h8 was not in the file because it was a very bad move, not a very logical one either. A lot of it of course was prep. But to spot a similar attack you don't have to be a genius.'

So less pleasing than one might have thought?

'It made me extremely happy, but if you compare it to beating Magnus or winning Tata it is going to be under that, so it has to be a 6.'

Two days after the Tata Steel tournament, Anish Giri and Jorden van Foreest appeared on Khalid & Sophie, a prime time chat show on Dutch TV.

Truly live

Wijk aan Zee is a highlight of the year for chess fans. Despite the tournament's long run and its reputation as a mecca for the game, the visit to watch the climactic final rounds was the first time I was on the spot to see the action truly live – and it is indeed an experience I can recommend to any enthusiast. The final round drama earned both Anish and 'wing man' Jorden van Foreest an appearance on one of the major national TV chat shows, and I was curious to learn if this level of interest in the game was unusual.

'There is a lot of interest in Wijk aan Zee and always has been. I got a lot of media attention when I became the youngest Dutch champion ever. And when I beat Carlsen as a 16-year-old in Wijk aan Zee. I remember in my school, only a few teachers knew something about chess, but they all knew there was this tournament in Wijk aan Zee. So this tournament is really followed in the Netherlands, but pretty much only this.

'Occasionally someone will recognize me but it's limited compared to other countries where I travel. I mean it's definitely bigger in Norway, in India it's huge. One of the surprising countries where I was recognized the most was Croatia. One evening I was walking around after dinner

with Aryan Tari, and I got recognized multiple times, it was very funny.

'But mainly I believe there is potential in Holland, we have good soil, Max Euwe and Jan Timman. It can be taken to another level at some point, but a lot of things have to come together first.'

Reflecting on Carlsen

I know from experience that introducing an element of psychology into a topic brings out the thinker in Anish. There were a number of moments at Tata Steel that really piqued my curiosity, but which took place on the inner landscape of the struggles, not on the board.

You were visibly wincing when people were congratulating you on the last day, with the word 'finally!'

'I think what they imply is that I have already been very close. They mean it well, that's for sure. If you take it out of context, 'finally' is something you say to someone who should have done it already, which is a compliment in a way too. I think even if they see it as having taken too long, it is a compliment, it is not a bad thing about the way they see you as a player in general.

'But as I always say, it also could not have happened this time. Unless you are really, really, really good, like

Carlsen has become, you're not going to win tournaments on demand. You have to be a little bit lucky. And I was lucky now. It could have been before, it could also not have been now.'

There was this very nice photo that appeared of you and Magnus, and you seemed to have a confused reaction to him congratulating you.

'Yeah, the one of us shaking hands. It's true, I didn't feel that to be a moment where he was as happy as he looked in that picture, but the picture is beautiful.'

There seemed to be an echo of a recent discussion around Magnus. When you beat him – and I know what you have said about him having plenty of time to accept defeat during the game – his reaction struck many as being unusually, if not uniquely, relaxed after a loss. Do you sense that Magnus may be mellowing?

'You have to wonder how genuine the way he expresses his emotions at that moment is. The other thing is that emotion comes with a delay, or sometimes the emotion changes. Something that I have a lot is: I lose, I feel a lot of pain just before I lose, then I feel OK while I resign, then I feel worse going to the restaurant, then I feel better having slept, and then I feel really bad again. So maybe he felt fine in that moment, and maybe he went back to the room and he felt awful about that loss.

'The other thing is that, from how I understand him, and I might be wrong – but I'm pretty sure I'm right – as someone who has to find the right motivation for the game. Because it is very hard for him – it is super hard when you are the world number one: you are in a very difficult psychological spot. You must have a constant fear of failure hanging over you. Because whatever you do is either a failure or not a failure. There is almost never an achievement for a World Champion, everyone expects you to win.

'He probably has to have mind tricks to help him stay at the top. One of the common ways of dealing with this kind of situation is you focus on the process and not the result. That is something that can easily keep him going forward, he doesn't care about the result, he sees the process. Then he can experience the failures and achievements that we who are not at the top experience, and not care about the result so much.

'What I guess happens a lot with his games is his emotion reflects him judging his process. You shouldn't over-analyse his emotions right after the game. Maybe he doesn't judge his games by whether he won or lost. That would make sense. If he judged his games by whether he won or lost he would probably feel awful his entire life because he either does what he should do or messes up.

'Unless you are really, really, really good, like Carlsen has become, you're not going to win tournaments on demand'

'Our game as a whole felt to me like he was still ready. I don't know if he spent a lot of energy on the preparation part, but he definitely was going for a fight and he spent a lot of energy at the board. So I don't know if he is mellowing or not.'

It is also hard to remember seeing him more disappointed than after he failed to beat Pragg in the penultimate round.

'That showed him being displeased with the process – because he made a lot of mistakes that he thinks he shouldn't be making. He was also clearly unhappy that it would mean the end of his chances to win the tournament. So I personally wouldn't say that I see the mellowing.

'I think the interview where he says he is fed up with classical chess mostly reflects him being very tired of the whole preparing thing. Maybe also playing, but I suspect the preparation routine is not to his liking; looking through the files, constantly choosing openings, not knowing what to play at some point because he always wants to surprise people, running out of ideas.'

A big year ahead

Let's focus on you. You have said that you didn't really feel Tata was the moment to celebrate, because it was not going to make or break the year or your career. This is going to be a big year. What are your thoughts on the title cycle and qualification – because you are presumably talking about a title challenge?

'Yes, a classical chess focus I guess. I am in a very privileged situation, where I can choose what game I want to play. I can make a pretty good living playing chess, or not. Or playing blitz or rapid or classical or whatever kind of chess. This year I think it is fun to play this whole FIDE cycle in classical chess.

'There are a lot of very good classical tournaments that have invited me – Wijk aan Zee, Norway Chess,

Anish Giri & Wijk aan Zee

Anish Giri has played in Wijk aan Zee 15 times ever since his debut in the C Group in 2009. Two years later he played in the top group for the first time.

Anish Giri is an official ambassador of the Tata Steel Chess Tournament.

2009	C Group	shared 2nd
2010	B Group	1st
2011	Masters	7th
2012	Masters	13th
2013	Masters	8th
2014	Masters	2nd
2015	Masters	2nd
2016	Masters	4th
2017	Masters	8th
2018	Masters	shared 1st
		loses play-off to
		Magnus Carlsen
2019	Masters	2nd
2020	Masters	6th
2021	Masters	shared 1st
		loses play-off to
		Jorden van Foreest
2022	Masters	4th
2023	Masters	1st

we've got the Grand Chess Tour, the World Cup, the Grand Swiss, and the idea of the FIDE circuit that counts every top tournament towards the Candidates standings. It motivates you even further in the cycle. Besides the rating that you are fighting for now, you've got a lot of (circuit) points.

'At the same time, coincidentally, the online events have shrunk to an enormous degree. Last year I had a major commitment to the Champions Tour. We also had a weekly rapid chess championship on Saturdays on chess.com for big prizes, we had the CGC (Chess.com Global Championship) as well, which was a big thing with giant prizes, bigger than the World Cup. You could focus only on online chess. Have all the

Chess Improvement with a Touch of Science and Philosophy

NEW!

Nick Maatman

THE HIDDEN LAWS OF CHESS

VOLUME ONE
Mastering Pawn Structures

NEW IN CHESS

The Dutch coach and International Master Nick Maatman is a sparring partner of super-GM Jorden van Foreest. He knows all about the level of understanding of titled players. But as a coach of regular club players, he also got to know what amateur players lack in knowledge.

Nick was looking for ways to bridge that gap and invented the Hidden Laws of Chess as an instructional tool to help his students. These Hidden Laws uncover elements such as space and the quality of a pawn structure.

Nick writes with a touch of science and philosophy. His book contains dozens of actionable tips, instructive games and carefully selected exercises. It will guide any ambitious chess player to the next level.

256 pages | paperback | €24.95
available at your local (chess)bookseller
or at newinchess.com

a **NEW IN CHESS** publication

fun and big prizes as well. It's much smaller now. You have six or something of these tour events, and it starts with a big Swiss, no one knows if you are there or not.

'It felt natural this year to shift the focus to classical. The cycle is there, the match without Magnus. It's fine, there are still two great players playing and the prize fund is there. Everybody's going to be watching. It would be interesting to try and see how it will go. Whether I succeed or not we will see, but the start is good. Why not try and keep it up?'

The title match

A general question is often quite fruitful when conversing with Anish. He has naturally pondered many of the chess world's talking points and you can tell when one appeals, as his speed of reply steadily accelerates (and his default setting is fast). There's a lot on his mind, and he wants to lay it out in detail.

What are your thoughts about the title match?
'Before Wijk aan Zee I thought that it was going to be a very interesting match because you have two players of roughly equal level. It's very hard to say who is the favourite.

'Nepo's got a clear advantage having had experience and seems to have a better organized routine. He always comes to a tournament with a second, well in advance, he has a big team of people, he knows how it's done. He knows what's important, he has experience winning two Candidates and also playing a match, knows how to allocate his time.

'Ding sometimes comes alone, maybe it's difficult to bring someone from China because of travel restrictions. He comes the day before the tournament, he often starts very badly because of that. So the opposite of what we see as professionalism. I don't know who is on his team, it might be a good one, but on the surface it looks like Nepo has

the team and experience advantage.

'Ding has shown better ability to bounce back from a difficult start. For example, in the Candidates he started very badly and he gradually came back to finish second. Nepo has had these famous meltdowns. Not only the match with Magnus, multiple other tournaments where things start to go badly and then he collapsed somewhat.

'So they have clearly asymmetrical strengths and weaknesses, and it's hard to estimate what is more important. After Wijk, we have to add that Ding was playing really badly, with mistakes not characteristic of his play. Maybe he wasn't able to focus on the tournament because of the upcoming match but it's not a good sign. You know how it is in chess, confidence is very important, the chances are high that you are not going to play well in the next event either. We'll see. In any case it will be an exciting match because we don't have a clear rating favourite, unlike when it was with Magnus.'

Less dramatic

Asking anything about the World Champion is guaranteed to produce some sharp opinions. So what does an ambitious Anish think about the title in a Magnus-less world?

'At first it seemed like a huge, huge deal because we are used to Carlsen being highest rated for a long long time. We got used to the fact that he is winning all the World Championships and many tournaments as well. But if we have time to cool off from the shock and excitement from him having withdrawn, I personally feel that it is less dramatic.

'Before Magnus became World Champion he was world number one when Vishy (Anand) was champion. We also had the time when Kramnik beat Kasparov, we even had these world champions from the knockout. Historically we've had lots of cases where there was someone higher rated or maybe stronger, but was

Magnus Carlsen congratulates Anish Giri on his victory. 'I didn't feel that to be a moment where he was as happy as he looked.'

not the World Champion. Such things happen.

'We also take it for granted that he will always be there as number one, but he still has to prove it. He constantly says he has no motivation for classical chess. He has some margin now, but it can go quickly. He might lose that spot in a year or two.

'For me it's a big question: what will his classical level be in the next five years? Because I think it is very difficult to maintain a high level without having the right motivation, especially in classical, because a lot is dependent on prep work. And psychology. If you are fed up and uninterested and don't want to prepare and you've got all these great talented youngsters who are super eager and also super good, it is not a given that he will stay number one forever.'

Because he will come down, or someone else will go up?
'Probably both, a bit like Fabiano (Caruana) did it. They'll meet at 2830.'

Swapping seconds

Time to air some potentially touchy subjects, the complications of losing and swapping seconds. As happened when Jorden van Foreest, who had

been regularly working with Anish, was enlisted by Magnus Carlsen for his title match against Nepomniachtchi. This led to friction between Anish and Jorden after the match. The role of assistants is both vital, given the crucial and complex nature of opening preparation, and somewhat shrouded in mystery. The composition of teams is also often slightly incestuous, since there are few who excel at the required skill set, and they are in great demand.

It seems that you didn't resume your collaboration after Jorden helped Magnus for the title match in Dubai, because he had some contractual obligations that prevented him from working the way you wanted? Were there some restrictions about openings or variations he couldn't discuss?
'I don't know the details of his contract. The short story is that we had agreed that he would work for Carlsen and that after the match he would be back on my team. When the match was over I was told that there were some restrictions, and so then he couldn't be back on my team.'

The natural question then is, why aren't there restrictions on your new second,

Jan Gustafsson, who has a longer association with Team Carlsen?
'I don't know. It might have to do with the fact that I wanted to work with him later than I wanted to work with Jorden? That might be a factor. Because I wanted to work with Jorden, February of last year. And my first tournament with 'Gusti' was this year, January.'

So you mean his restrictions might be lifted now?
'Maybe. I don't know. I can tell you one thing. I can tell you that when I asked Jorden he said he had restrictions, and when I asked Jan if he was allowed to work with me, he told me he was. Jorden and I have good relations and there was never a personal problem, there was just a decision at some point that we were unable to work with each other professionally because of the restrictions that are on him.'

And I suppose this has an obvious answer, but how is the new collaboration working?
'The fact that the event went so well is representative of neither my chess level nor the quality of our work. I'm

not that great, the work is not that good (laughs).

'We have a long way to go, and there are lots of things I have to work on. I'm far from satisfied with my level of preparation, my form in chess, but in Wijk it worked out pretty well. But I'm not going to say that this is the dream team that's doing great things. Lots of things can be improved throughout the prep process. Which is always the case.'

Can you say something about the way they work, how they are different?
'Yeah, they are very different and the role that they play in my team is very different. Erwin (l'Ami) has been my main coach for many years and he's been there throughout everything. He is still very much there. The issue we always had is that at Wijk aan Zee he is playing as well, so he can never be my second there.

'Also I felt it was never enough just to work with one person, so for many years I have had a dynamic team, that changes. For the Candidates I have a specific team because that's an event for which you can prepare for very precisely and for which you should allocate more resources than usual. I can't afford to have a full-time team the entire year, the costs are too high.

'Jorden is very creative, a very outside-of-the-box kind of guy. He's young, compared to me at least, and very much in touch with the tech and the engines. He's really good working with engines in a modern way and he's also very good with tech in general, with computers. He's very often a little too out of the box for me, and for Magnus as well. Many of his ideas are out of my comfort zone, I find them too complex to navigate,

'Jorden is very creative, a very outside-of-the-box kind of guy'

more downsides than upsides, but still it's fantastic to have someone like that.

'Like everyone, he has advantages and disadvantages. When you are this creative you have less order, because if you have more order, you kill the creativity. If you only had Jorden as a second, you'd have a lot of loose ends in the files, things that are unfinished.

'One of the most ordered people I have ever seen is probably Kramnik

(Anish Giri was on Vladimir Kramnik's team for the 2018 Candidates Tournament in Berlin – ed.). We got hit in one of the games in the Candidates, because of this. The way he works is so ordered, he wanted to look at all the moves, literally, methodically. First he outlined all the moves, and said, let's look at them one by one. And by doing that, he created a structure for me in which I was not given a chance to find an alternative. And finally we got hit by a move that was not on the list because he didn't realize it was an alternative at all. He created a framework for me where I was not allowed to find what was outside the framework, and we got hit by that novelty. So it works both ways.

'With Jan (Gustafsson), it is very different. Right now he is my second. Jorden never went with me to tournaments, he was on my team, not my second or coach. I was with Jan throughout Tata. He wasn't with me to find the weirdest ideas. They do different jobs within the team, so I didn't replace Jorden with Jan, that's not what happened. If anything Jan's role is more that of Erwin's.'

They also play a personal role?
'Yeah, of course. When you are at a tournament it is very beneficial to

have someone as company. There are a lot of dinners, you have someone you can discuss your losses and your wins with.'

Were you looking to get a Carlsen second?
'There are a very limited number of professional coaches, seconds, so you are going to get this situation. I needed a second and had limited options, there were only a couple of candidates that could meet my very difficult list of demands ☺.

'One of the criteria was that the person had to have a lot of experience working at the top level before. It's special to find someone who is available to work a lot. I was fortunate to find someone who has the time, who is good on a personal level, and has a lot of experience at the Candidates or World Championship level. That he has seconded Carlsen before, or would have seconded Anand, or Kramnik or Caruana, that is not important.'

The evolution and future of the game

With chess enjoying a series of booms, gaining a higher profile as an e-sport, the form of its evolving public appeal can be seen as both boon or bane for the game. The showpiece of the new breed of speedier top-level events is the 2023 edition of the online Champions Chess Tour. It has a much broader format this year, with hundreds of players eligible to try and play their way in to a multi-division knockout, a step towards the democratization of big events. How does this strike Anish?

'The format is a good example for sure, for other organizations as well. But it isn't going to change the entire chess infrastructure, let's not exaggerate. A few extra thousand euros a year for some 2600 players, it isn't a salary. More people earning is a good step towards democratization but you need more sponsors. I think it's a pyramid, the money comes from the

top down. I don't think a sponsor is going to come and fund specifically 2600 players.'

But money tends to stay at the top...
'The way I see chess becoming democratized is the top becoming overcrowded. If you have tournaments clashing with each other, 30 a year, then a top player will play ten of them, and then organizers will have to start looking at the top 20, and if

> '**You can make a strong case for classical and for rapid. In terms of money and attention it is very close**'

these are also busy then maybe top 30. And that's how democratization starts. They would discover some of the players outside this circle are also gifted. I think this is the way it would have to go.

'The FIDE circuit will stimulate players to play in more events, but the eventual winner will be someone who plays closed tournaments, because I think they are higher weighted. The way to go is to overcrowd the calendar.'

You don't see the absence of Carlsen affecting the status of classical chess, especially with what looks like rapid on the rise?
'Now there is a classic tournament like Wijk aan Zee that he hasn't won, and then there is this interview where he says he is fed up with classical chess. Then it looks more like it is him going away from it.

'The trend was definitely shifting to rapid, but this year... it's close

right now. There are really good prizes in classical chess – the World Championship, they play for millions. The online tour prize money this year is distributed very, very well, across many players, which is a great thing they are doing. There are a lot of reasons to think that chess goes rapid, because in general everything that is good in the world gets faster, definitely. A great argument, but you can always say counter to that, that chess is a very specific game based on tradition. Whenever I see people that don't know anything about chess, they always ask, 'How long do your games last?' And when they ask that, they expect a long answer. They expect you to say five hours, seven hours, and then they say 'Wow!' They know that that's coming, deep inside they know it is long, they associate chess with something that lasts forever.

'You can make a strong case for classical and for rapid. In terms of money and attention it is very close. I saw a graph the other day, the most viewed events. First was the World Championship, then the Candidates, then Pogchamps. Right now in terms of money and viewership it is very close between rapid, blitz and classical. What matters more is, I think, very subjective.'

You're still a very firm believer in the vitality of classical chess...
'Yes, but we are relying on a few big things. It could fall apart if FIDE plus big sponsors and the top players collectively decided to abandon it. But it seems that FIDE is ruled by reasonably traditional people, and the players, OK, Magnus doesn't like it, but others like Nepo, Ding and Fabi don't seem to mind ☺.

'Again, the World Championship, the Grand Chess Tour, Wijk aan Zee, Norway Chess, Dusseldorf, the Olympiads and team events are all being funded well. And there is interest. So it seems the rumours of the death of classical chess are somewhat exaggerated.' ∎

Moving Up

Alexander Donchenko wins Tata Steel Challengers

The Tata Steel Challengers was a two-horse race with Mustafa Yilmaz and Alexander Donchenko setting a stiff pace. On the final stretch, the German GM broke away, winning his last four games to claim promotion to the 2024 Masters.

Alexander Donchenko's victory in the Challengers had all the makings of a charming fairy-tale. Two years ago, the German grandmaster made his debut in the Masters(!) in Wijk aan Zee as a last-minute substitute for Daniil Dubov. After the initial excitement, the windy village unfortunately didn't extend much of a welcome. Due to the pandemic, the 14 Masters were the only chess players in a small ghost town. All public life had come to a forced standstill, and the chess players were largely confined to their hotel rooms. The rounds were long and tough, and drawing seven games and winning none, Donchenko finished last. 'I had played top players before, but not 13 in a row. That was a unique experience.'

Many lessons were learned and one of them was that you have to bring a second for such a tough test lasting over two weeks. For him the choice was easy. 'I brought my mother with me. She is the best second you can have, as she is obviously someone I am very comfortable around. She knows what I like and what I don't like. And she's someone I can tell to leave me alone when that's how I feel.'

Donchenko had an encouraging start, winning half of his first six games – but so did Mustafa Yilmaz. The Turkish number one had arrived in Wijk aan Zee in an optimistic mood, feeling that this field offered him good chances, provided he was in good form. Yilmaz had come alone,

> '**Where it will take me, I don't know. But at least I will get 13 games against the very top of the chess world**'

but felt the strong support from his friends at home and the 'amazing Turkish fans' that expressed their support in various manners.

The first big clash was the direct encounter between the leaders in Round 7, which ended in a fine win for Donchenko (see his notes to that game below). Now he was the sole leader, a point clear of the runner-up, but his comfort was short-lived. In the next round, Yilmaz reduced the

gap with a win against Uzbeki super-talent Javokhir Sindarov (see his notes below) and in Round 9, Donchenko slipped up in a rook ending against Erwin l'Ami (see Jan Timman's column on rook endings).

Looking at the programme for the final four rounds, Yilmaz felt that he had good reason for renewed optimism, but as it was, the story took a completely different turn. While he himself missed winning chances in two games, Donchenko proved to be super-alert after his wake-up call against l'Ami. First he fully regained his self-confidence with a win as Black against the solid Max Warmerdam, and then went on to win his other three games as well.

For Mustafa Yilmaz, the final few days were a cold shower that left him with mixed feelings. 'I am not sure if I should feel happy or upset. If you'd told me before I came here that I would score 9 out of 13 and win 20 rating points, I'd be so happy... But now I feel as if I've missed an opportunity and I can only hope that one day they will invite me again.'

For Alexander Donchenko, drawing conclusions was easier after winning the right to play in the Masters for a second time. 'I can definitely say

Finishing first in the Challengers, Alexander Donchenko earned the right to try his luck in the Tata Steel Masters again and wipe out the memory of his last place in 2021.

that this is the biggest victory so far in my career. Where it will take me, I don't know. But at least I will get 13 games against the very top of the chess world – which is already a whole lot. If it gets me more, I'd be even happier, but so far I am already very happy that I have qualified for next year.' *(DJtG)*

NOTES BY
Alexander Donchenko

Alexander Donchenko
Mustafa Yilmaz
Wijk aan Zee Challengers 2023 (7)
Queen's Gambit Declined, Ragozin Defence

This game was played in Round 7, after I had just caught up with Mustafa Yilmaz on 4/6. The tournament was not even halfway done, but obviously both of us understood that this game would be crucial for the final standings.

1.d4 ♘f6 2.c4 e6 3.♘f3 d5 4.♘c3 ♗b4 The Ragozin Defence is my opponent's main opening. On the upside for me, I play the Black side of it as well, and it was a relatively predictable choice, making my preparation easy.

5.♕a4+ ♘c6 6.e3 0-0

7.♕c2!? I had not played this before, but I saw the game Caruana-Gukesh earlier in the event, which inspired me to take a closer look at the line. It turns out that many subsequent positions give fighting chances, while

remaining strategically sound, which suited me for this game.

The other main line is 7.♗d2 dxc4 8.♗xc4 ♘d6 9.♕c2 e5. I had this position with both White and Black in classical games, but the theory is just beginning here.

7...b6 The aforementioned game went 7...♘e7 8.♗d2 b6 9.a3 ♗xc3 10.♗xc3 ♗a6 11.b3, and Caruana soon enjoyed a large advantage.

8.♗d2 ♗b7 9.cxd5!

This is White's main strategic idea against ...♗b7. The bishop will be passive for now and the c7-pawn is a potential target. On the other hand, Black will control the e4-square and have several ways to become active on the kingside.

9...exd5 10.a3 This bishop is Black's most important piece for his kingside play, so it makes sense to gain time by attacking it.

10...♗d6 10...♗xc3 11.♗xc3 ♕d6 12.♗d3 is very passive for Black, who will struggle to create activity on the kingside.

11.♘b5 ♗e7 12.♗d3 a6 13.♘c3 ♗d6 14.0-0

After a number of natural moves we have reached a position that has occurred in several (GM) games. Yilmaz chose the most natural regrouping and was still following my preparation.

14...♘e7 The knight is heading for g6, so all of Black's pieces are starting to close in on my kingside.

The computer points out 14...♖e8 15.b4 ♘b8! as an alternative. The point is to improve the queenside knight compared to the game, where it ended up very passive: 16.♖fc1 ♘e4 17.♗e1 ♘d7, with counterplay.

15.b4!

As ...c5 is a common way for Black to get rid of the backward pawn, I naturally make it harder for him. The move is also part of my strategic plan on the queenside, which will be revealed in the game.

15...♘g6

With 15...c5?! Black would have traded the weak pawn by force, but at the cost of leaving his position full of holes: 16.bxc5 bxc5 17.dxc5 ♗xc5 18.♖fb1 ♖b8 19.♘a4 ♗d6 20.♘c5 ♗xc5 21.♕xc5, and White is clearly better.

16.b5!

This move is the only effective way to generate play on the queenside. The c7-pawn is fixed in place (for now) and I am preparing a lengthy manoeuvre to trade the dark-squared bishops via a3. The idea is obviously not new and was even played in this very position, so Yilmaz still has plenty of decent options to deal with it.

16...♖e8!? Yilmaz keeps the tension for the moment and makes it hard for me to decide on his intentions on the queenside.

I think that 16...a5?! is a little too committal: 17.a4! ♕e7 18.♕b3 ♖ad8 19.♗c1 ♘e4 20.♗a3, and White is much faster with his plan than in the game.

The most direct move is certainly playable: 16...axb5 17.♘xb5 c5 18.♘xd6 ♕xd6 19.♖fb1! ♗a6. This was seen in Babula-Alekseev, World Cup 2021. After 20.♗xa6 ♖xa6 21.a4 Black had a lot more freedom, but he still needs a few moves to neutralize White's queenside play completely.

17.♖fc1 a5

My own rook is in the way of ♗c1-a3 now, which should be a small achievement for Black.

18.♘e2

My knight is heading for g3, the most effective square at the moment.

18...♘e4 19.♗e1

Black's position appears very active, but in reality he has to be careful not to run out of ideas on the kingside.

19...h5?! After this, Yilmaz will struggle to maintain the tension without hurting himself.

Both 19...♕f6 20.♘d2 h5 21.♘f1 h4 22.h3 ♖ad8 and 19...♘h4!? 20.♘e5 ♘f5 21.♘f4 g6 22.♗xe4 dxe4 23.♕c4 ♕e7 were slightly better ways to proceed, because they would maintain Black's firm control of the e4-square.

20.♘g3

I obviously have to play this move before ...h4 prevents it.

20...♘xg3

During the game I expected 20...h4!? 21.♘f5 ♖c8! 22.♘xd6 cxd6, when Black will be forced to give up his important bishop, although his light-square play might make up for it: 23.♕d1 h3! 24.g3 ♕f6 25.♗f1 ♖xc1 26.♖xc1 ♖c8 27.♖xc8+ ♗xc8 28.♘d2.

The last few moves were semi-forced, but Black's pawn weaknesses are still much harder to exploit now.

21.hxg3 ♛f6 I thought I had made big progress with the knight trade, but things are not so simple.

22.♗c3

As long as I can prevent his ...h4 push, I have time to finally execute the dream bishop trade via a3.

22...♖ad8 The computer points out 22...h4!!. I did not seriously consider this sacrifice, but White's static advantage on the queenside makes it necessary. Whatever I try, the black pieces are still too active to claim any advantage:

– 23.gxh4 ♞xh4 24.♞e5 ♛h6!, with the idea of ...f6.

– Black has good compensation for the pawn after 23.♗xg6 fxg6 24.♞xh4 ♖e4! 25.♞f3 g5 26.♞e5 g4.

– And has counterplay after 23.g4 ♗c8 24.♗xg6 fxg6 25.♞e5 ♗xe5 26.dxe5 ♛g5.

23.a4 ♗c8 23...h4!? was still possible, but here it is less strong than before: 24.♗xg6 fxg6 25.♞xh4 ♖e4 26.♞f3 g5 27.♗b2 g4 28.♞e5, and White is only marginally better.

24.♗b2 ♗g4

25.♞h2 A good alternative was 25.♗xg6!? fxg6 26.♞e5 ♗f5 27.♛b3, but I was perhaps fixed on the ♗a3 idea too much.

25...♗e6?!

Now ♗a3 will come with a lot of force.

Clearly best was 25...♞e7!, even though I did not think so at the time. In the game, this knight will be hindering Black's coordination. After 26.♗a3 ♖c8 27.♛b3 ♛e6 Black still has weaknesses, but for the moment they are hard to attack properly.

26.♗a3!

Finally the long strategic plan has come to fruition. And in this particular position, Black will be unable to deal with this trade, mostly due to the poor knight on g6.

26...♖c8

Since 26...♗xa3?! 27.♖xa3 ♖c8 28.♖c3 will lose the pawn in the long run.

27.♛d1

Compared to 25...♞e7 Black's second weakness on h5 is now hurting as well.

27...h4 28.♗xd6 cxd6 29.g4

A much more direct approach was 29.gxh4!? ♞xh4 30.♖c6! ♛g5 31.♗f1. However, I had already assessed the structure in the game to be strategically winning and wanted to avoid unnecessary risks.

29...♞e7 30.♖xc8

One major piece is enough to exploit the c-file, and Black cannot contest it due to his (yet again) misplaced knight.

Initially, I had intended 30.f4 g5 31.f5 ♗d7, but then I realised there was a

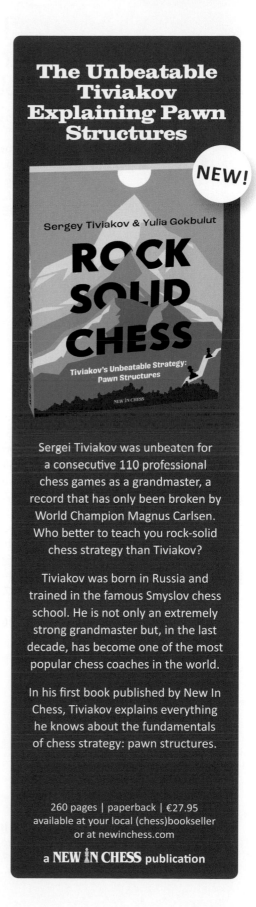

possibility of a fortress, so I decided to keep this option for later.

30...♖xc8 31.♗c1

31...g5 A waiting move like 31...♔f8 32.♖xc8+ ♘xc8 33.f4 will not stop my expansion.

32.♖xc8+ ♘xc8 33.♕c2!

The perfect square for the queen, as we will see.

33...♔f8

Yilmaz is just one move short of covering his weaknesses.

Bad was 33...♕d8?! 34.♗f5 ♕d7 35.♗xe6 ♕xe6 36.♕c7, as it immediately lets the queen dominate the position.

34.f4!

I was really happy to find this move, but as usual, the computer sees an alternative.

Also winning was 34.♗f5! ♔e8 (34...♗xf5 loses after 35.gxf5 ♘e7 36.♕c7! ♘xf5 37.♕xb6) 35.♗xe6 ♕xe6 36.♕c7 f6 37.♔f1 ♕d7 38.♕xd7+ ♔xd7 39.f4 ♔e6 40.♘f3.

However, 34.♕c7?, or any other slow move, would allow Black to defend: 34...♔e8 35.♔f1 ♕d8.

34...♕e7

After 34...gxf4, 35.♕f2! is the point, of

'I felt that the game followed a clear strategic thread from start to finish'

course. Suddenly the action switches to the kingside and the black knight again plays a tragic role: 35...♔g7 36.♕xf4 ♔e8 37.g5, and White wins.

35.♔f2

I am not rushing things. The threat of f5 cannot be parried, so I improve my position slowly.

35...♕f6

Also losing was 35...gxf4 36.exf4 ♕f6 37.♔e3! ♕e7 38.♔f3 ♕f6 39.f5.

Most resilient was 35...♕d8!?, but here we see the benefit of keeping the structure flexible: 36.♗f5! (36. f5? ♗d7 37.♘f3 f6 could very well be the fortress I was afraid of) 36...♗xf5 37.gxf5 gxf4 38.f6! fxe3+ 39.♔xe3 and the domination strategy is complete.

36.f5!

I had to make sure that Black could not get back to the set-up after 35...♕d8, and here he will not be in time.

36...♗d7 37.♕c7 ♕e7 37...♔e8 is met by 38.♘f3 ♕e7 39.♕b7, winning.

38.♕b7 The d5-pawn cannot be defended. **38...f6 39.♗c2**

Patience pays off. Black cannot move, which is more important than the pawn count. Of course, the immediate 39.♕xd5?! wins as well. However, there is no reason to allow 39...♗e8!? 40.e4 ♗f7 41.♕c6 ♕d8 42.♘f3 ♘e7 43.♕b7, when there is still some work to be done.

39...♔e8 40.♘f3 ♔d8 41.♕xd5 ♗e8 42.♗b3!

Keeping Black paralysed.

42...♕d7 43.e4 ♘e7 44.♕a8+ ♕c8 45.♕a7 ♕c7 46.♕xc7+ ♔xc7 47.e5

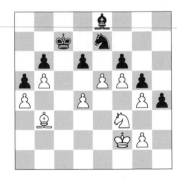

The bishop on b3 restricts the minor pieces, so all the pawns on the kingside will eventually fall. Black resigned.

I felt that the game followed a clear strategic thread from start to finish. But as is always the case afterwards, both sides had several opportunities to break that flow to their advantage. This victory earned me the sole lead and a tie-break advantage over my closest rival.

NOTES BY
Mustafa Yilmaz

Mustafa Yilmaz
Javokhir Sindarov
Wijk aan Zee Challengers 2023 (8)
Réti Opening

Playing the Tata Steel Challengers was an important opportunity for me to show myself, and from the beginning of the tournament I only wanted to win this event. After Round 6, I had 4/5 points and was sharing first place, but unfortunately I lost a crucial game against Alexander Donchenko in the next round and I slipped down to third place.

Going into this game, I had mentally prepared myself for a big fight and was ready to take risks to beat Javokhir Sindarov, who was in 2nd place.

1.♘f3 ♞f6 2.c4 g6 3.♘c3 ♝g7 4.e4 e5

The Dubov Tango was the name of this line, according to Peter Svidler, a name I had never heard of. This one came as a surprise. He has been mainly playing the King's Indian.

5.♘xe5 0-0 6.♘f3 ♜e8

7.♝d3

This approach should be the safest. I guess that what Black is hoping for is 7.d3, after which the play could continue 7...d5 8.cxd5 ♞xd5 9.♝d2 ♝g4 10.♝e2 (the game Giri-Dubov, Moscow 2019, saw 10.♕b3 ♞xc3 11.bxc3 ♞a6 12.♝e2 ♞c5 13.♕c2 ♝xf3 14.gxf3 ♕h4 15.d4 ♞e6 16.♕c1 c6, with an edge for Black (½-½, 36)) 10...♝xf3 11.gxf3 ♞b4 12.♝e3 ♞8c6 13.a3 ♞a6 14.h4 ♞d4 15.h5 ♞c5, with compensation for the pawn. For a human, this doesn't look so easy to play.

7...♞xe4 8.♝xe4 ♝xc3

I spent some time trying to understand 8...f5?, which was not in my notes, and calculated 9.d3 ♝xc3+ 10.bxc3 fxe4 11.dxe4 ♜xe4+ 12.♝e3, when Black's king is very weak and White is up for preference.

9.dxc3 ♜xe4+ 10.♝e3

10...d6?!

Black should start with 10...♞c6, even if after 11.0-0 d6 (now c5 won't work because Black can capture the pawn) 12.♕d2 ♜xc4 13.♝g5 ♕e8 14.♜fe1 ♝e6 15.b3 ♜c5 16.c4 the rook on c5 looks very bad and Black's king is quite weak again.
Clearly bad is 10...♜xc4? 11.♕d5.

11.c5

I couldn't remember my notes, but I did remember that there was c5 somewhere, and I thought it should be here. I knew that So had won an easy game against Mamedyarov, but I couldn't recall the details.

11...d5 12.0-0?!

12.h3, not allowing ...♝g4, was called for here. I hesitated between 0-0 and h3, and picked the wrong one. After 12.h3 the play could continue 12...b6 13.0-0 ♝b7 14.b4 ♞d7 15.♞d2 ♜e6 16.♞b3. White will slowly bring his pieces into the game and Black has no active plan.

Wijk aan Zee Challengers 2023

				1	2	3	4	5	6	7	8	9	10	11	12	13	14		TPR
1	Alexander Donchenko	IGM	2627	GER	*	1	½	1	1	½	½	1	0	1	½	1	1	1	10	2787
2	Mustafa Yilmaz	IGM	2609	TUR	0	*	1	1	½	½	½	1	1	½	½	1	1	½	9	2719
3	Javokhir Sindarov	IGM	2654	UZB	½	0	*	½	½	½	½	½	½	1	1	1	1	1	8½	2684
4	M. Amin Tabatabaei	IGM	2686	IRI	0	0	½	*	½	½	½	½	1	1	½	1	½	1	7½	2629
5	Velimir Ivic	IGM	2585	SRB	0	½	½	½	*	½	0	½	½	0	1	1	1	1	7	2609
6	Adhiban Baskaran	IGM	2610	IND	½	½	½	½	½	*	1	0	1	½	½	½	1	0	7	2607
7	Luis Paulo Supi	IGM	2608	BRA	½	½	½	½	1	0	*	½	½	½	1	0	1	½	7	2607
8	Max Warmerdam	IGM	2616	NED	0	0	½	½	½	1	½	*	0	1	½	1	½	1	7	2606
9	Erwin L'Ami	IGM	2627	NED	1	0	½	0	½	0	½	1	*	½	1	½	0	1	6½	2576
10	Thomas Beerdsen	IM	2515	NED	0	½	0	0	1	½	½	0	½	*	1	½	1	½	6	2556
11	Abhimanyu Mishra	IGM	2559	USA	½	½	0	½	0	½	0	½	0	0	*	½	1	1	5	2495
12	Rameshbabu Vaishali	IM	2425	IND	0	0	0	0	0	½	1	0	½	½	½	*	½	1	4½	2482
13	Eline Roebers	IM	2361	NED	0	0	0	½	0	0	0	½	1	0	0	½	*	½	3	2386
14	Jergus Pechac	IGM	2637	SVK	0	½	0	0	0	1	½	0	0	½	0	0	½	*	3	2365

12...♗g4!

He spent 48 minutes on this move ☺.

13.♕b3

And I spent almost half an hour on this one.

My backup plan was 13.h3, but I never felt as if White was exerting pressure here. After 13...♗xf3 14.♕xf3 ♘d7, I thought that if he brought his knight to e6, the position would be equal.

13...♘c6?!

He had to start by destroying my kingside: 13...♗xf3 14.gxf3 (we both calculated the forced line 14.♕xb7?? ♖g4 15.g3 ♕h4 – the computer is in no rush ☺ and finds 15...♘d7 – 16.♕xa8 ♕h3 17.♕xb8+ ♔g7, and I'm getting mated) 14...♘e5 15.♕xb7 ♘d7. I guess we both failed to understand this position. Black has enough compensation for the pawn.

14.♘d4

14.♘d2 was also good.

14...♘a5

15.♕b5

My initial plan was 15.♕c2, but I don't know why I changed my mind after every single move. The pressure was probably affecting me: 15...b6 16.♗h6 bxc5 (after 16...♗d7 17.b4

♘c4 18.♕c1 White has a permanent advantage: f3 is coming) 17.f3, and White is winning.

15...b6

After 15...c6 16.♕d3 ♗d7 17.b3 b6 18.♘e2, he'll end up with a very weak king and not enough activity.

16.c6?!

Analysing this game with an engine makes me feel very bad. This move was very risky. I couldn't understand what was going on, because he had so many options, but I told myself that if this one worked, it would restrict his pieces, so I could play for a win. If not, what to do...?

White is better after 16.♖fe1 a6 17.♕b4 ♘c4 18.♗h6.

16...♕d6?!

Missing the chance to play 16...♘c4! 17.♗c1 a6 18.♕a4 ♗e2! (an important resource) 19.♖e1 ♕e7, and I might get into trouble soon.

17.♗g5!

Now the threat is f3.

17...f6 18.♗c1!

It looks really strange that I returned my bishop to the first rank. It's all about keeping f3 in the position. Black has no way to stop it, and all

his pieces have to go back, leaving me with a huge space advantage.

After 18.♗h6? ♗f5 Black threatens ...♖h4, with a double attack.

The immediate 18.f3 was very unclear to me, e.g. 18...♗xf3 19.gxf3 ♖xd4 20.cxd4 fxg5 21.♖ac1 ♖f8.

18...♗f5 19.b3

Starting with 19.f3 would have been better, but I never thought about touching my rook on f1. And the engine says that after 19...a6 20.♕a4 ♖ee8, 21.♖d1 is the only move to have an advantage.

19...a6

20.♕d3

What I wanted was 20.♕a4, followed by ♗a3 and ♗b4 and starting to grab some material. At the same time, having the queen out of play was scary. I was afraid of getting mated: 20...♖ae8 21.♗a3, and now:

ANALYSIS DIAGRAM

21...♕e5 is the computer's suggestion: 22.♗b4 ♖g4 23.♗xa5 ♖h4 24.g3 ♗h3 25.gxh4 ♕f4 26.♘e2 ♕f3 27.♘f4 ♖e4 28.♘xh3 ♖g4+ 29.♕xg4 ♕xg4+ 30.♔h1 ♕f3+, and perpetual check. I was more worried about 21...♕f4 22.♗b4 (22.f3 wins for White)

Mustapha Yilmaz: 'If you'd told me before I came here that I would score 9 out of 13 and win 20 rating points, I'd be so happy... But now...'

22...♕h6 23.♗xa5 ♖h4 24.h3 ♗xh3, and Black wins. It was these kinds of lines that made me play 20.♕d3.

20...♘xc6 21.♘xf5 gxf5

Here, neither of us had much time left, with still quite a few moves to be made to reach move 40.

22.f3

I considered 22.♗a3, but it wasn't enough: 22...♕d7 23.♖ad1 ♖d8 24.♕xa6 ♘e5, which favours Black.

22...♘e5??

This normal-looking move is losing. He should have played the more solid 22...♖e7, when after 23.♕xf5 ♕e6 24.♕h5 ♕f7 25.♕h4 ♘e5 26.♗d2 ♘g6 27.♕g4 ♖ae8 Black should have good chances to hold.

23.♕c2 ♖h4 24.♕xf5

Now I am winning. Nothing will work here for Black.

24...♖xh2 The alternatives are equally hopeless: 24...♘xf3+ 25.♖xf3 ♕xh2+ 26.♔f2, and White wins.

'I am very happy with my performance, and the experience will be remembered forever'

24...♘g4 25.fxg4 ♕xh2+ 26.♔f2, and wins.

24...♖e8 25.g3, and the rook on h4 is trapped.

25.f4

Now Black suffers a big material loss. After this he still tried a bit, but with a rook less there is not much you can do.

25...♖xg2+ 26.♔xg2 ♘g6 27.♕h3 d4 28.♗d2 ♔h8 29.♖ae1 dxc3 30.♕xc3 ♖g8 31.♔f3 ♘e7 32.♔e2 ♘d5 33.♕f3 ♕c6 34.♖c1 ♕d7 35.♗d1 ♘b4 36.♖c4 ♖d8 37.♕c3

Here I wanted to repeat once, 37...♕g4+ 38.♕f3 ♕d7, and then play 39.♕e2, but he blundered immediately and I finally won the game.

37...♘d3 38.♕xf6+

Black resigned.

After this victory I went on to win another game and took the lead again with 6/9, but Donchenko won his last four games and I couldn't keep up with him. In the end, I took second place in the Tata Steel Challengers. I am very happy with my performance, and the experience will be remembered forever. ■

WHAT BUSINESS TAUGHT ME ABOUT CHESS

Deliberate Practice vs Deliberate Play

When my first business was almost bankrupt we considered switching our business model from making websites for large companies to making tea. Like, tea that you buy in a store and then heat up and drink.

That year (1995-1996) we made the first websites for AmericanExpress.com, TimeWarner.com and many others.

We charged a lot of money. But it's hard to get clients like that. I'm not so good at following up on emails so it was very hard for me to wine and dine decision makers for months, go to their charity events and kids' baseball games and, on top of it all, respond to their emails and phone calls.

I hated it.

For a week, my partners, employees, and I would bring in a new tea each day that we made. I can't even remember how I thought of ideas for teas. Trust me when I say that we all felt like throwing up after trying all the teas brought in each morning.

We didn't go into the tea business.

Then I had an idea. Let's start a record label. It'll be easy. We just find a musician who hasn't been discovered yet, we pay for studio time, and we get radio stations to play their music.

No problem!

We found one rapper we liked. On the World Wide Web. We called him and said we wanted to be his record label.

He said, 'Uhhh, who are you guys again?' He had no record label but he turned our generous offer down.

Then we thought about writing TV shows. We shot one episode of a show where we would secretly videotape people who were on blind dates.

And we thought about making an 'internet cemetery' – websites for dead people. I made a website I called 'the Internet Beauty Contest', where people could post pictures of themselves, and others can vote if the entrants were beautiful or not.

I even called up various beauty or celebrity magazines to see if they would sponsor us.

Ultimately we continued to make websites and two years later we sold the company to a bigger company that then went bankrupt when everyone figured out they could make websites without hiring a company to do it.

Was it a waste of time to make tea? Or try to make a record label? Or write TV shows? Of course not!

■ ■ ■

The first period of my chess life was from the ages of 17-18 and then from the ages of 27-28. I took a break for college. And, like many aspiring young chess players, I took a break to explore the fashion business (kidding – but that's exactly what one 2785 rated player is doing now).

I was obsessed with openings. It was all I studied. This was in the late 80s and then in the 90s.

I only played the 1.d4 recommendations in Raymond Keene's now outdated book *An Opening Repertoire for White*.

Basically, he recommended systems with d4 and, sooner or later, ♘ge2-g3 and then either breaks with e4-f4-f5 or h4-h5 (in both cases, supported by the knight on g3).

And then, as Black, I played 1...g6 no matter what. My bibles were *The Modern Defence* by Vlastimil Hort and *The King's Indian Defence* by Efim Geller.

I would study a chapter, then try to make index cards from memory of the variations. I have better memory

Was it a waste of time to make tea? Or try to make a record label? Or write TV shows? Of course not!

now of things I memorized when I was 18 years old than if someone asked me what I had for breakfast this morning.

The famous '10,000 hour rule' states that if you do 'deliberate practice' in whatever field interests you, you will become an expert in that field.

Deliberate Practice means – Do the task, Analyse (with a coach ideally), then Repeat. Do – Analyse – Repeat.

Professor Anders Ericsson, who coined the rule, studied violin players, memory world champions, tennis players, and even chess players (in the early 90s I participated in some of his experiments on chess players).

I spoke with Anders shortly before he passed away. He thought people didn't really understand what the 10,000 hour rule was so he wrote a book called *Peak* to summarize all his research.

'The deliberate practice part is key. You have to repeat and repeat and repeat the skills of your area and each time, study what went wrong, then repeat. Chess is perfect for this.'

Study tactic after tactic. 1000 tactics about pins. About skewers, forks, etc. Study the opening, play it, fix, repeat.

But as I return to tournament play 25 years later, I realized something: not only do I not have 10,000 hours available to study, but it completely doesn't work for me. I was miserable and losing.

■ ■ ■

When I looked at my most recent 500 games I realized a few things. In the games I lose:

A) I often get a good game out of the opening
B) I hardly get into an endgame
C) I make bad decisions in the middle game, that lead to bad positions, that lead to bad tactics
D) I lose

A blunder is hardly ever an accident. It's like when a spouse cheats on his wife or her husband. 'It was an accident!' is never an excuse.

There are a thousand things that have to happen. Your spouse has to meet up many times with the 'cheat-ee'. Whispers are exchanged. Hotels are booked. Separate phones might be bought. Messages hidden. Lies exchanged.

And then, finally, the 'blunder' occurs.

From left to right: Me, professional comedian Jim Norton, GZA from the Wu-Tang Clan, a local amateur chess player named Garry Kasparov, and poker player Maria Konnikova.

What was going on in my games that was making me make such poor choices that they would finally add up to a blunder?

■ ■ ■

Why was it worth it that we tried to make a tea company.?

That we tried to start a record label? Or an Internet Cemetery (a social network for dead people) and on and on.

We must've false-started a dozen businesses instead of just focusing on our real business. Our real business was ultimately the one that succeeded and none of the other ideas worked. We wasted 100s and 100s of hours. What a waste.

Or was it.

After we tried and failed to start a record label we started to pitch REAL record labels that they needed websites (nobody had websites back in 1995-1998, the years of our business).

We ended up doing the websites for Loud Records (the Wu-Tang Clan), Bad Boy Records (Puff Daddy), Jive

Records (Britney Spears), all of Interscope's record labels and many more.

25 years later I played a chess match against the GZA from the Wu-Tang Clan. He's pretty good!

And the hundred hours or so we spent on creating TV shows that never aired? Well, we ended up doing the websites for HBO, New Line Cinema, Miramax (yes, that Harvey Weinstein), and movies like 'the Matrix', 'Scream', and hundreds of others.

And what about all the effort spent on making 'The Internet Beauty Contest'? Which, was sort of like a social network since people could follow, email, like, post 'diary posts', etc about the entrants and anyone could be an entrant.

Well, a decade later I made a site that was a social network for investors, Stockpickr, which I sold to thestreet.com when we hit a million users a month.

Am I saying that because I was exposed to all of these different ideas, it made my business better? No. What made the business better was that I was having fun.

I was getting burnt out pitching JP Morgan on why they needed a website. I hated being nice to clients I didn't like. I hated being yelled at by middle management marketing executives.

I hated being fired by a client. I hated firing employees. I just didn't enjoy the business.

But I loved making a new kind of horrible tea every morning.

Or trying to find a musician for our new record label. And we did film a few TV shows. They never aired but they were so much fun to do.

And yes, I learned things. I learned a great deal about things I was curious about. And I learned I had more options than I thought when it came to business.

I had switched from repetition (programming websites, making sales calls, returning calls, going to useless meetings), to play.

Injecting fun and play into the business was the only thing that kept it alive.

■ ■ ■

I wasn't having fun in the middle game.

As I was going through my games I could viscerally remember what was going on when I got to that point when the opening was over and the middle game was starting.

I would tense up. My shoulders would move about an inch higher. I'd start thinking to myself, 'if I don't do this exactly right I'm going to lose, and I hate losing.'

I would look at these games afterwards and think, 'Man, I had a great attack going. Why didn't I just sac here? Or

bring another piece around? Why did my piece suddenly go on an adventure to the other side of the board?'

I got obsessed with my online rating going up every day. I would think to my casual blitz games with friends, where

Deliberate Play is to take the tried and true path that you study all the time and throw in a twist

I was just having fun. So many more attacks and fun sacrifices. BOOM! BAM!

I wasn't doing Deliberate Play. I was too focused on Deliberate Practice. Make the right moves, analyse, repeat.

So I started to do Deliberate Play.

What would happen if I play 1.a4 followed by 2.h4? These are considered so bad – would I just lose instantly? I couldn't possibly play that!

But why not?

Deliberate Play is to take the tried and true path that you study all the time and throw in a twist.

By regularly doing Deliberate Play you expand your options and you increase your knowledge of the kinds of things that work, or could work, or don't work. And, by the way, most directions your curiosity will take you, will work.

Even the computer agrees with this.

Do you know that after, 1.a4 d6 2.h4 g6 the computer says the position is +0.4 in favour of White?

I was watching Hikaru's 'Disrespect Speedrun' on Twitch and he sometimes starts with these two moves. Is he truly disrespecting his opponents with these moves?

Many questioned Hikaru's return to tournament chess in the recent Candidates tournament. 'He's just a streamer now!' was a common critique.

But maybe he was doing a massive amount of Deliberate Play. Eight hours a day of playing unusual openings (the Bong Cloud!) and getting into wild middle game positions that these other 2700s had never encountered.

The result? He was a solid contender to win the Candidates. And then he won the World Championship for Chess960!

Deliberate Play not only made him a fun streamer to watch but it made him a better chess player! A World Champion.

Deliberate Play has worked for me over and over in business and investing. I am not a natural business person and I don't often enjoy it. So following my curiosity and asking 'What if I did...?' as much as possible, often makes me a better businessman.

What if I just write to Google and give them some ideas? What if I just go to a sales meeting and only recommend they hire my competitors? What if I do a Kickstarter to raise money to buy Greenland?

What if I take my podcast and turn every episode into a mini-book I self-publish on Amazon? What if I then offer that service to every podcast out there – to turn their episodes into books for them so they can have an alternative stream of income for their podcast. Nobody has done this. Sounds like a fun business idea to try!

I've started doing Deliberate Play more in my online chess (I haven't yet tried in over the board).

It's more fun, more relaxing, and instead of always playing what I think is 'the right move' I play often the 'What if I try this move, it looks interesting...?' and then I see and learn from what happens.

Chess is not a repetitive skill. It's a game. It's fun. It rewards curiosity.

Chess is not a repetitive skill. It's a game. It's fun. It rewards curiosity

If you are like me, someone trying to get better as an adult (after a 25-year break), here are some fun experiments to try.

– Take your black openings and play them as White. (When you play 1.e3 nobody will have any idea whether you are playing a reverse Dutch, or reverse French, or a reverse Hippo, or if you are just going crazy.)

– Try exchanging all of your pieces as quickly as possible. You'd be surprised that even if the exchanges seem to have no point, how many of your opponents simply collapse in the endgame.

– Sometimes I try to play 'no ambition chess'. Just make moves that are safe, with no real plan other than to slightly improve a piece and then wait and see what the opponent does. Sooner or later they try too hard (ambition!) and blunder.

– Research some weird opening (a4/h4!) and play it.

– The next 20 games, gambit a pawn in the first few moves (but not the Queen's or King's Gambit).

– Just try attacking the side *without* the king and see what happens. At least for me, I got addicted to only attacking on the side where the king was. Then the attack would often fail and I'd be miserable. Relieve the pressure on yourself.

– This was suggested to me by GM Avetik Grigoryan (and this exercise is featured in his course 'Saving Lost Positions' on ChessMood.com). In each game, sacrifice a piece on the second move. For instance, 1.e4 e5 2.♗a6 !

This takes the pressure off (because now you are totally lost) but you fight like hell to activate your pieces and try to swindle a win.

I was surprised how many games I won and it gave me confidence in positions I would normally be despondent in.

■ ■ ■

In 1997 I stopped playing tournament chess because one of my business partners told me, 'why are you obsessing on some game? You should be focused on making more money in your business. Take business more seriously!'

And I did. I stopped chess. I took my business more seriously and I was miserable. Every time in life when I took business seriously I was miserable. Only with Deliberate Play did I find any success in business.

And now I am bringing it back to where it started. I realized I was taking my chess too seriously and that has been hurting my results.

I want to do more Deliberate Play to explore my curiosity more in chess, understand better the range of options I have that I never realized I had in positions familiar to me, and get better at the parts of the game I never even looked at.

I think this will improve my game and widen my understanding. Chess is too vast to explore on the path well-trodden. So far, so good.

But that's not why I do Deliberate Play. I do it because I want to have fun playing this game I love. ■

James Altucher has written 25 books. About 21 of them are bad but one or two are OK. He has started several companies and has a popular podcast called 'The James Altucher Show'. Among others, Garry Kasparov and Judit Polgar have been guests on his podcast, as well as Kareem Abdul-Jabbar, Richard Branson and 963 others. He has played chess since he was 16 but stopped when he hit 2204 USCF in 1997, and is now starting to play again.

Aronian flawless in tiebreak

American bounces back to win WR Chess Masters

At the age of 40, he may well be considered an 'elder statesman' of the game, but Levon Aronian rolled back the years by claiming victory in the WR Chess Masters in Düsseldorf. Truth be told, he had to win the event twice after a false draw claim cost him dearly.

by JOHN HENDERSON

T he WR Chess Masters was a surprising newcomer to the elite-scene. Held at the upscale Hyatt Regency Hotel – sadly, on-site spectators were not welcome – the event came hard on the heels of the Tata Steel Masters and contained seven of the same faces in the 10-player round-robin.

Düsseldorf cannot boast of a rich recent chess history, but the city's past claim to chess fame includes four games of Emanuel Lasker's successful World Championship title defence against Dr Siegbert Tarrasch in 1908.

The tournament was created as a warm-up event for Ian Nepomniachtchi – who, just like other Russians, was not welcome in Wijk aan Zee – ahead of his coming World Championship match against Ding Liren. The sponsor was his chess-loving entrepreneurial friend, Wadim Rosenstein – hence the 'WR' initials in the title – CEO of the WR Group. German citizen Rosenstein was originally born in Russia, and through his Düsseldorf logistics company retains considerable business interests there by supplying Western equipment and expertise to Russian industry.

The field was a mix of different generations and styles, and it was not only interesting to see how Nepomniachtchi would fare, but also if one of the top teenage talents would make a big splash. As the games got going, it proved to be Levon Aronian who proceeded to steal the show, sprinting to a commanding lead after six rounds. Having defeated Praggnanandhaa in Round 1, Aronian also beat Nodirbek Abdusattorov in Round 3 with an old idea against the Dragon.

NOTES BY
Jan Timman

Levon Aronian
Nodirbek Abdusattorov
Düsseldorf WR Masters 2023 (3)
Sicilian Dragon, Yugoslav Attack

1.e4 c5 2.♘f3 d6 3.d4 cxd4 4.♘xd4 ♘f6 5.♘c3 g6 6.♗e3 ♗g7 7.f3 0-0 8.♕d2 ♘c6 9.g4
After the game Aronian observed: 'I played the Dragon until I turned 16. This g4 is not very popular, but it's

The tournament was created as a warm-up event for Ian Nepomniachtchi ahead of his coming World Championship match

kind of tricky, and I'm not sure that my opponent was aware of this move'. And indeed, Abdusattorov would not be long to drop a stitch.

9...h5

The usual move is 9...♗e6. The text was first – and last, actually – played at grandmaster level in Dolmatov-Dorfman, Tashkent 1983. It is rather dangerous to provoke White on the kingside like this.

10.g5

Dolmatov went for 10.h3 in order to maintain the tension on the kingside. Black can then try to create some counter-pressure in the centre with 10...

d5, possibly resulting in sharp play, as witness 11.g5 ♘h7 12.♘xd5 ♘xg5 13.0-0-0 ♘xd4 (13...♗xd4) 14.♗xg5 ♘xf3 15.♕b4 a5 16.♘xe7+ ♔h7 17.♕b3, and now Black has the queen sacrifice 17...♕xd1+ 18.♔xd1 ♘xg5, with compensation.

With the text, White closes the kingside and starts playing for a space advantage. A very good alternative was 10.gxh5 ♘xh5 11.0-0-0, intending to launch an attack.

10...♘e8

A new move, and a surprise for the commentators. This retreat is

probably slightly stronger than the more common 10...♘d7.

11.0-0-0 ♕a5

The computer indicates the modest 11...♘c7 as its first choice. After 12.♔b1 ♗d7 (or 12...♖b8) Black seems to be cramped, but he has a concrete plan: aiming for ...b7-b5, and it will not be easy for White to exploit his space advantage.

12.♘b3!

Forcing a queen swap in favourable circumstances.

12...♗xc3 13.♘xa5 ♗xd2+ 14.♗xd2

14...f6? An incomprehensible move. It seems as if Abdusattorov has neglected to take sufficient account of the move 10.g5 during his preparation. The general rule about not opening the game if your opponent has the bishop pair applies here, too. The active 14...♘d4 was Black's best option. There could follow: 15.♗g2 b6 16.♘b3 ♘xb3+ 17.axb3 a5 18.♗e3 b5, and now 19.♔d2!, opening the a-file for the queen's rook, is strong. White is better.

15.♘xc6 bxc6 16.gxf6 ♘xf6

How Black recaptures is of no consequence. After 16...♖xf6 17.♗g5 ♖xf3 18.♗xe7 the black position collapses.

17.♗h6 17.♖g1 ♔h7 18.♗e2 would also have won. **17...♖e8 18.♗c4+ ♔h7 19.♗g5 ♔g7** More tenacious was 19...♘d7, meeting 20.♖hg1 with 20...♘e5 21.♗e2 a5, when White can afford to allow a bishop swap, since 22.♖df1 ♗a6 23.♗xa6 ♖xa6 24.f4 ♘g4 25.h3 ♘f6 26.e5 ♘e4 27.f5! would give him a decisive attack.

20.♖hg1 a5

21.♖g2 White is going to double rooks on the g-file, while Black can only watch.

21...♘d7 22.♖dg1 ♗a6

Or 22...♘e5 23.♗e2 ♗a6 24.♗d1!, and White wins.

23.♗b3 ♘f8

24.♗d2 En route to c3. **24...♗c8 25.a4 e5** Now the d-pawn will get irreparably weak, but there was no alternative.

26.♗c3 ♗e6 27.♖d2 The rooks are doubled on a central file.

27...♗xb3 28.cxb3 ♖e6 29.♖gd1 ♖d8

30.f4 The decisive breakthrough.
30...g5 31.f5

Black resigned.

■ ■ ■

Now an on-song Aronian always gives entertaining reasons when he hits a purple patch. This time, he revealed on the live stream, that he was binging his way through the 1980s miniseries *Berlin Alexanderplatz*, Rainer Fassbinder's 15-hour odyssey through the seedy underbelly of 1920s Berlin. And with the interwar plot being so sad 'that it makes me happy as soon as I can sit at the board again. Everything is quite wonderful then.'

Everything was indeed quite wonderful for Aronian, who looked to be cruising to a comfortable victory. Thanks to a third win against

					1	2	3	4	5	6	7	8	9	10		TPR
	Düsseldorf WR Masters 2023															
1	Levon Aronian	IGM	USA	2736	*	0	½	½	½	½	1	1	½	1	5½	2810
2	Ian Nepomniachtchi	IGM	RUS	2793	1	*	½	½	½	1	½	½	½	½	5½	2804
3	Gukesh D	IGM	IND	2718	½	½	*	½	½	½	½	½	1	1	5½	2812
4	Wesley So	IGM	USA	2766	½	½	½	*	1	0	½	½	½	½	4½	2727
5	Jan-Krzysztof Duda	IGM	POL	2729	½	½	½	0	*	½	½	½	½	½	4	2688
6	Vincent Keymer	IGM	GER	2690	½	0	½	1	½	*	½	1	0	0	4	2692
7	Anish Giri	IGM	NED	2780	0	½	½	½	½	½	*	½	½	½	4	2682
8	Nodirbek Abdusattorov	IGM	UZB	2734	0	½	½	½	½	0	½	*	1	½	4	2687
9	Andrey Esipenko	IGM	FIDE	2675	½	½	0	½	½	1	½	0	*	½	4	2694
10	R Praggnanandhaa	IGM	IND	2690	0	½	0	½	½	1	½	½	½	*	4	2692
	Aronian won the 3-way blitz tiebreak															

Assessing Aronian's clear wish to draw, Ian Nepomniachtchi took a decision that blew the tournament wide open again.

Anish Giri, he held a full-point lead going down the homestretch. Three draws was probably all he needed for first place – but then came his fateful Round 7 clash with Nepo, who had thus far slumbered his way through the tournament with six relatively uneventful draws. For Aronian a welcome draw seemed to be in the making, and it did not feel like he objected to the idea.

Levon Aronian
Ian Nepomniachtchi
Düsseldorf WR Masters 2023 (7)

position after 19...♗d8

20.♕c5 ♗e7 21.♕b6 ♗d8

22.♕c5 ♗e7 23.♕b6
Here Aronian claimed a three-fold repetition – which was a false claim as they did not reach the same position for a third time – and Nepo decided to up the ante by pressing on both physically and psychologically with some three-fold teasing in-between moves.
23...g5 24.♗g3 ♗d8 25.♕c5 ♗e7 26.♕b6 f5

Aronian is still angling for a draw – but Nepo is clearly feeling he now has the psychological advantage.
27.f3 ♗d8 28.♕c5 ♗e7 29.♕b6 ♗d8 30.♕c5 f4 31.exf4 gxf4

32.♗f2 ♗e7 33.♕b6 ♗d8 34.♕c5 ♗f6 35.♖fc1 ♕g7 36.♕d6 ♖ce8 37.♖e1 ♘e5

38.♘d4? Not so easy to see, but the only way to hold on was 38.♔f1!, side-stepping all Black's tricks.
38...♗h3! The tactics are all now winning for Nepo.
39.♗f1 ♘f7 40.♕xd5 ♖xe1 41.♗xe1 ♗xd4+ 42.♔h1 ♗c8
And with Aronian a piece down, Nepo went on to easily win (0-1, 53).

As Nepomniachtchi commented after the game: 'I felt like maybe if he wants a draw that badly, then I should push.'

That cruel loss unexpectedly blew the tournament wide open. It allowed rising Indian teenage star Gukesh to catch up with Aronian. With highly inventive and adventurous play he beat Andrey Esipenko in the same round.

Nepomniachtchi: 'Maybe if he wants a draw that badly, then I should push'

NOTES BY
Jan Timman

**Andrey Esipenko
Gukesh D**
Düsseldorf WR Masters 2023 (7)
Catalan Opening, Closed Variation

**1.d4 ♘f6 2.c4 e6 3.♘f3 d5
4.g3 ♗b4+ 5.♗d2 ♗e7 6.♗g2
0-0 7.0-0 c6 8.♕c2 ♘bd7 9.b3
b6 10.♘c3 ♗a6 11.e4 dxc4
12.♖fe1 e5**

A sharp move, that was introduced in the game Panjwani-Lee, Charlotte 2022.

13.♘e2! The best reaction.
13...♘g4 This is new. In the aforementioned game 13...cxb3 14.axb3 ♗xe2 15.♖xe2 ♕c7 16.♗c3 followed and White had a big advantage.

14.bxc4

The critical move appears to be 14.♗c3. It's not clear to me what Gukesh was planning here. The computer sees nothing better than 14...f6. There may follow 15.♖ad1 ♕c7 16.♗h3 and now Black will have to support the knight with 16...h5. It doesn't look reliable for Black, but

I assume Gukesh had prepared this down to the last detail. The advantage of a line that is not highly valued by the computer is that you can lure your opponent into unknown territory.
14...exd4 15.♘exd4 ♘de5

16.♘xe5

After this exchange, White no longer has a chance to gain a positional advantage. White could immediately play his bishop to c3 (again), but 16.♗f4 was also possible. After 16...♘xf3+ 17.♘xf3 ♗c5 18.♖e2 f6 White is better according to the computer, but the position is not entirely clear. Black also has his trumps.
16...♘xe5 17.♗c3 ♗c5 18.♖ad1 ♕c7

Now Black has solved all opening problems.

19.f4

A sharp pawn sacrifice. With 19.♘b3 ♗a3 20.c5 White could have led the position into calmer waters.
19...♘xc4 20.♔h1 ♖ad8 21.♘f5
The point of the pawn sacrifice. White has attacking chances.
21...f6 22.♖xd8 ♕xd8

23.♕e2

A curious mistake. White should have pinned the knight by 23.♗f1 and has enough compensation for the pawn. The game can get sharp, as evidenced by:
– 23...b5 24.g4 ♖f7 (on 24...♗c8, 25.♗xf6 is again possible) 25.e5 fxe5 26.fxe5 ♕d5+ 27.♕e4 and White has sufficient compensation for the pawn thanks to the strong e-pawn.
– 23...g6 24.♗xf6! ♖xf6 (after 24...♕xf6 25.♗xc4+ ♗xc4 26.♕xc4+ ♔h8 27.♘h4 White has an advantage) 25.♗xc4+ ♗xc4 26.♕xc4+ ♔h8 27.♘h4 g5 28.♘f5 gxf4 29.gxf4 ♕d2 with sharp play and roughly even chances.
23...g6!

Suddenly White stands empty-handed.
24.♘h6+
White didn't have good squares for the knight. The alternative 24.♘h4 was not sufficient either. After 24...♗d4 25.♖d1 c5 26.♘f3 Black has the hammer blow 26...♘e3!.
24...♔g7 25.♘g4 ♗d4
Simple and strong.
26.♖d1 c5
Black supports his bishop, so that he gets all the trumps.

27.♕f3 The black knight's pin does not work in any way to White's advantage, e.g. 27.e5 fails to 27...♘xe5!.
27...h5 28.♘f2

28...♘e3 Sticking to his plan. The computer gives 28...♘e5. White's queen is almost captured and after 29.fxe5 fxe5 30.♗xd4 exd4 31.♕a3 ♗e2 White has nothing to hope for.
29.♖d2 ♕c7 30.♗xd4 cxd4
31.♖xd4 ♕c3 32.♖d7+ ♖f7
33.♖xf7+ ♔xf7

It is equal materially, but the activity of the black pieces gives Gukesh a decisive advantage.
34.h4 More tenacious was 34.h3, to control square g4. Black then liquidates to a won endgame with 34...♕e1+ 35.♔h2 ♕e2.

LENNART OOTES

Gukesh remained true to his dynamic style, spoiling for a fight in each game.

34...♗c4 35.♗h3 f5!

The fastest way to victory. White is bricked in.
36.♔h2 ♕d2 White resigned.

■ ■ ■

Going into the final round, Aronian and Gukesh – both fighting back admirably after their patchy performances in Wijk aan Zee – shared the lead on 5/8. However, just half a point behind there now lurked a reinvigorated Nepo.

Both co-leaders then went through the motions of playing out a tame 18-move draw in Round 9 to be assured of a play-off for the title. And just when everyone thought that Nepo would need a 'miracle' to beat local hero Vincent Keymer from a totally equal ending to join them in the playoff club-

house, one did turn up with a blunder at the end of their near six-hour game. As a result, a three-way playoff was to decide the outcome of the title.

But all's well that ends well, as perhaps Shakespeare would say, as Aronian this time made no slip-ups. Oozing confidence, he raced to a perfect 3/3 to claim the €40,000 first prize and the inaugural WR Chess Masters title ahead of Gukesh and Nepomniachtchi. ■

COLOPHON

PUBLISHER: Remmelt Otten
EDITOR-IN-CHIEF:
Dirk Jan ten Geuzendam
HONORARY EDITOR: Jan Timman
CONTRIBUTING EDITOR: Anish Giri
EDITORS: John Kuipers, René Olthof
PRODUCTION: Joop de Groot
TRANSLATOR: Piet Verhagen
SALES AND ADVERTISING: Edwin van Haastert
© No part of this magazine may be reproduced, stored in a retrieval system or transmitted in any form or by any means, recording or otherwise, without the prior permission of the publisher.

NEW IN CHESS
P.O. BOX 1093
1810 KB ALKMAAR
THE NETHERLANDS

PHONE: 00-31-(0)72-51 27 137
SUBSCRIPTIONS: nic@newinchess.com
EDITORS: editors@newinchess.com

WWW.NEWINCHESS.COM

Bruce Pandolfini on the set of The Queen's Gambit with Anya Taylor-Joy, the star of the Netflix miniseries. 'The most important thing is that you look like you're really playing chess.'

Bruce Pandolfini:

'I wouldn't know why Bobby wouldn't be up there now'

Over the past half century, he has coached outstanding talents like Fabiano Caruana and Josh Waitzkin, but he also built a clientele of Wall Street hotshots, world leaders, business tycoons and film stars. Thanks to his talent for hard work and his love for the game, Bruce Pandolfini can look back on a totally unique career. It all started with the Fischer-Spassky match in 1972, and it never stopped. An interview about his gift to be at the right place at the right time, his involvement in *Searching for Bobby Fischer* and *The Queen's Gambit*, the chess game between Messi and Ronaldo, and much more.

by DIRK JAN TEN GEUZENDAM

In his book *Searching for Bobby Fischer* (1988) Fred Waitzkin describes how, once or twice a week, Bruce Pandolfini would turn up at 6.30 in the morning for a training session with his son Josh. As I cite the early hour, Pandolfini smiles at the memory. 'Yes, I would do that. I would frequently work from 6 in the morning to 2 in the morning. I was younger then, I didn't need as much sleep as others. I certainly needed two to three hours, but I could do it on that.' After a small pause he adds, 'You may ask, who takes lessons at midnight? Well, you'd be surprised. There are artists, musicians, chess players! Ladies of the night. All kinds of people took lessons after midnight.'

He still has a working schedule, but at the age of 75 it is about half of what he used to do. 'Maybe 20, 25 hours a week. Usually one or two sessions in the morning, three or four throughout the rest of the day. Much of it is done by Zoom, but I still like going to people's homes and offices. That was always part of the charm and lure of the business.'

Bruce Pandolfini speaks from his home in New York via Skype, seated in front of a wall of books. Chess and books have always been two corner stones in his life. He specifies that the books he has around him are only a fraction of his total library. The biggest part is kept in five storages around town. The storages cost him more than the place where he lives. Besides chess, the books at his home mainly belong in the categories of history, literature and philosophy. Furthermore, his love for *Ulysses* cannot be left unmentioned. At the instigation of a fellow-member of the Marshall Chess Club, he read James Joyce's magnum opus for the first time when he was 17 – and understood little of it. Right now he is reading it for the 21st time. He doesn't see himself as an expert, but feels that for an amateur he knows quite a lot.

Actually, it was thanks to books that Pandolfini's chess career got an unexpected – and as it turned out life-changing – impulse more than a year after he had played his last tournament game as an active player in 1971.

'I was a national chess master, but not an outstanding player. I might have gone further, but it didn't seem like a practical thing for me and I was putting all my efforts in being a writer at the time, perhaps a poet. That didn't go anywhere. I was working in the Strand Book Store, a big and famous book store in New York. This was 1972, and this man came to the counter and placed five

The improbable success of Shelby Lyman's show during the Fischer-Spassky match essentially started Bruce Pandolfini's coaching career.

A publicity photo from around 1980 with a clear message.

Fred Waitzkin watches on as Bruce Pandolfini and Josh Waitzkin are constructing a game that should work as the very last game in *Searching for Bobby Fischer*.

chess books on it, which he wished to purchase. We had a brief conversation, and a few days later he calls me. He was a producer, and he says, would you like to be an analyst on Channel 13 for the Fischer-Spassky match? And I said, what? He so liked what I had to say in those few minutes about chess and on the books he was buying. And that's how I got back into chess.'

Pushing Sesame Street off the air

The programme on the match was presented by Shelby Lyman, a master from New York. Contrary to the lukewarm expectations, it became an improbable success and turned Lyman into a national celebrity. At some point, the show was so popular that it temporarily pushed Sesame Street off the air. 'I knew Shelby and he did tell me he was going to cover the World Championship match. I thought, that's ridiculous, no way could you put that on American television then. So I was his assistant, a very small role, but so many people watched that it impelled me to a chess career.'

The next step was that Shelby Lyman got him into chess teaching. 'One

day, after one of the shows, he said, I don't have any time, could you give a lesson to one of my students? And I said, I am not a chess teacher. And he went, I am going to teach someone now, why don't you come along and see how it's done? So I did. This was a newcomer, a gentleman who had never had a chess lesson before. And Shelby says to him, let's play a game. And the student says, but I don't know how the pieces move. And Shelby says, move them the way you think they move. And I thought that was profound. Obviously, the student couldn't divine how the pieces moved, but he was so focused after that. And he picked it up much quicker after this. I thought, this is a field I could get involved in, teaching chess; and it took off from there.'

It was the Fischer-Spassky boom in 1972 that drew Pandolfini back into chess, but looking at the milestones in his long career, it is remarkable how most of them were directly or indirectly connected to Bobby Fischer. His role in *Searching for Bobby Fischer* introduced him to a

larger audience; first his prominent presence in the book (1988) and then in the movie (1993) where his part was played by none other than Ben Kingsley. *The Queen's Gambit* tells the story of the chess career of Beth Harmon, but everyone understands that this story would never have been written if Walter Tevis had not seen Bobby Fischer in action. Here, too, both the book (1983) and the Netflix hit series (2020) with Anya Taylor-Joy profited from Pandolfini's chess insights and expertise.

Stanley Kubrick and Billy Wilder

The first time he actually met Fischer was in 1963, when Pandolfini was 16 years old. Bobby Fischer was 20. 'Grandmaster Larry Evans was giving an exhibition at the Marshall Chess Club and I was one of the combatants, and my game wound up the last one left. I was Black in a Sicilian, and I didn't play very well. Evans won a pawn and he finally ground me down and I had to resign. But suddenly, before the end of the game, as I was the last one left, he sat down in a chair and suddenly I was facing Evans

Viktor Korchnoi meets Congressman Charles Pashayan in Washington in 1977. On the right Lev Alburt and Bruce Pandolfini, who hoped Korchnoi would settle in the US.

directly. For the last 10 minutes, Bobby Fischer had come into the club and he stood right behind me. I think he was going to go out with Evans and have dinner. They were good friends, or very friendly associates. Eventually I resigned. The spectators gave Evans a huge hand, he signed my scoresheet and somebody said, Bobby should sign the scoresheet too. But he had started running away, he didn't like signing things. But as he was leaving the Marshall, he was grounded by Carrie Marshall, Mrs Frank Marshall, and she could get anyone to do almost anything. "Bring him back to the board!", and "Bobby, sign the kid's scoresheet!" That was my first encounter with Bobby Fischer.'

Several months later he would again watch Fischer from up close, when he scored his historic 11-0 win in the 1963/64 US Championship and Pandolfini acted as a wall boy, moving the pieces on the demonstration board next to Fischer's table. Again, and not for the last time, he was at the right place at the right time.

'Absolutely! I've worked very hard.

Many people don't realize that. But I was also very lucky. I handled five of Fischer's games at that 11-0 championship. The big one, as far as I remember, was his game against Reshevsky. At that game, seated in front row, were two great film directors, Stanley Kubrick and Billy Wilder, who were chess fans. I didn't know what they looked like, but that's what I was told. Fischer was great news, even then.'

He'd run into Fischer at times, but they never became close. 'Fischer was always friendly to me. I wasn't a friend of Bobby's, I don't pretend that.

'Once I sat with Fischer and analysed for three hours, chess games from various European journals. That was a trip'

He had very few friends. But I had a number of conversations with him. Once I sat with him and analysed for three hours, chess games from various European journals. That was a trip. But I couldn't have called him up on the telephone and say, let's go out, you know. The friends he had, that I knew of, were Jackie Beers, who I think he lived with for a short time, Bernie Zuckerman, and maybe a couple of others. Plus, I looked up to him as a god. Just to be even next to Fischer for a few seconds was an honour. Nor did I ever play him a game, not even a speed game. If I had, believe me, I would say it.'

Stimulating the imagination

Right from the start of his coaching career, Pandolfini had a serious approach. 'I kept notes on all my students; I wanted to be scientific about it. I have journals going back to 1972. Some of it is fascinating, most of it isn't, of course. Just ordinary entries, what a student did on that day and possibilities. I have entries on people like Max Dlugy, who I gave endgame lessons to, Joel Benjamin. I must have worked with a dozen people who became grandmasters. They did it on their own, because of who they are. People think that teachers help make a student, but I think students make a student. Maybe a teacher can open a few doors or encourage them. I always try to show my love for the game. That's what I could do to inspire my students, and I did that quite well. Most of my students have been newcomers or relative newcomers, and I think I am fairly adapted to that, I have so much experience with it.'

He agrees when I suggest that rather than expecting his pupils to memorize and repeat material, he tries to stimulate their imagination, so that they keep thinking of what they are actually doing.

'Yes, that's a very good way of saying it. I try to make people more mindful of their actions, to understand their reasoning, their logic. Chess is a game of logic, but it's also a very intuitive game. It's a game that draws upon many talents, actually. As any serious chess person knows, there's not one thing you have to do. Chess players do many things, from trying to visualize things in the future to changing their approach when they realize a situation is shifting, when you must suddenly think differently. Much of that can be modified and adapted to help you in other areas. And so I try to instil in my students a sensitivity or feeling for those ways of looking at things, so they can use them whatever they do. Besides being good chess players.'

'In the beginning I didn't know how to go about it. I did have to develop a regimen. I had the feeling that I was a good endgame player, so I would start with endgame material as recommended by the greats, such as Lasker, Tarrasch, Capablanca. Of course, real endgame play doesn't have to do with the big mates. It has to do with converting an extra pawn to a win or stopping that. So I would present those positions, but I would be insistent on one thing and that is, you weren't allowed to move the pieces. Because I think a student has to acquire that ability somehow. Otherwise, how do you play chess? And if a student touched a piece and made the correct move, he was marked wrong, because I wanted to make sure that they would never touch a piece again. You had to learn how to analyse in your head.'

World leaders and actresses

Due to his inability to say no and his insatiable appetite for work, Bruce Pandolfini's chess activities have always been diverse and widespread. ('I was always fortunate to have surprising things happening in my life.') He has been the Executive Director of the Manhattan Chess Club, the Director of the Chess School of the Marshall Chess Club, and has always been a prolific writer

In 2001 *The New Yorker* published a photo of Bruce Pandolfini and 8-year-old Fabiano Caruana, shot in Washington Square Park. On the right the 2015 remake.

and columnist. Yet, the core business remained his work as a coach. As his fame and reputation kept growing, one is inclined to believe that through the years, for instance after his appearance in *Searching for*

'Chess is a game of logic, but it's also a very intuitive game'

Bobby Fischer, his hourly rates must have gone up. When I draw that tentative conclusion, he laughs and reacts immediately.

'The rates were high from the very start! To my mind, the best chess teacher around in America in 1972 was Shelby Lyman, and I am not talking about his television show. Prior to that, he had at least a dozen private students and a couple of classes at chess houses and even at school levels. He was actually making a living of it. And he charged 12 dollars an hour for a private lesson, which was very high

in '72. So Shelby advocated that I charge 15 dollars an hour! And I said, Shelby, that's ridiculous, I am not even a grandmaster. He was a very strong player, but he wasn't a grandmaster either and he said, no, no, you start at 15 dollars an hour. And of course I did that, and it quickly jumped to 20 an hour, 25 an hour, and it just mushroomed. It was ridiculous. And I helped other professionals get their rates up. There were strong players charging a dollar an hour. What are you saying if you charge one dollar an hour? This is a worthless activity? Why are you doing that? It's not only bad for you, but also for the rest of us.'

Right from the start, his students included famous and well-known names who expected privacy and discretion, an expectation that he still abides by. 'There were reasons for that. If they looked bad or unintelligent, they were very concerned with that. So I had to keep all that secret. I kept all my private sessions secret, but I took painstaking notes. I felt like a kind of therapist, you know, an analyst of some kind, almost like a medical doctor. Because so much of what I was teaching involved getting inside the minds of the students. I could ask questions, hundreds of questions during the hour, trying to get a sense of who that individual was, so I could present material and help them better. I have very detailed personal notes and I never thought it proper to share any of that. But there were some very famous people. You'd be amazed. From world leaders to famous actors and actresses, artists.'

What has never been a secret is that easily his most famous student was Fabiano Caruana. They worked together for almost two years between 1998 and 2000, and the memory comes with another remarkable Fischer reference.

'Well, how could I top Fabiano? (laughs) I would see him once or twice a week. We analysed his games, other great games with themes pertinent to what he was doing, what he needed to cover. And we studied the endgame exhaustively. Smyslov and Levenfish, books like that. There was a Polish endgame series I used to use. I had a few books that came from Bobby Fischer's collection. That I could acquire in a quite remarkable way. When I was 16 years old, I was working in a bookstore and Fischer came in, because he knew the owner, and he needed some money. Here's the great Bobby needing money. He sold a bunch of books, maybe for 200 dollars, to the owner of the store. And when Fischer left, I immediately said, can I buy some of those books? It cost me two weeks of salary to buy four books, but they were well worth it. They were signed. There was the Lipnitsky book that Fischer became a grandmaster on, the actual copy. It's obliterated, the spine, but I have it. Just like I have a comic book of Bobby Fischer's that he translated from Spanish into English, writing underneath each line... a very rare piece.'

On the set of *Searching for Bobby Fischer*, the real Bruce Pandolfini instructs Ben Kingsley, who plays Pandolfini in the film, how to make his chess play look real.

Largest chess package ever

Pandolfini has written many chess books, but he feels he lacked the time for a real masterpiece. 'I've always wanted to write one really good book, but it's so hard. At one point, I had to write nine books in two years. It is ludicrous. Yes, that was the Fireside Chess Library (which he started in 1983). Simon & Schuster wanted to replace the Reinfeld, Chernev and Horwitz titles. Those were irreplaceable, I feel, for what they set out to do. They really brought chess out in such a lively wonderful manner. Anyhow, I couldn't turn down the package of

> 'The world's greatest teacher, all blah-blah-blah, I've nothing to do with that. That's the advertising department.'

the nine books, which I sold without an agent. When I did get an agent later, she said to me, I've never known anyone to sell a series of books on their own to Simon & Schuster. How did you do that? I'm a good salesperson, I guess. It was certainly the largest chess package ever.

'But I am not a natural book writer, I had to work hard. Each one could have been done better, but I always do so many things, all my days were packed. I wish I hadn't been so superficial. I know I could have done a better job at points, but I didn't. This is life. Once it's out there, there's nothing you can do. As far as the book covers, the world's greatest teacher, all blah-blah-blah, I've nothing to do with that. That's the advertising department.'

The books were a commercial success, but not everyone was impressed. Chess historian Edward Winter checked the books for historical accuracy and published a list of errors. Pandolfini does not blame him. 'That's OK, I deserved it. He was correct. The attack was painful,

Lionel Messi (photographed in Paris) and Cristiano Ronaldo (photographed in Manchester) check the engines' assessment. 'Ah, good, it's a draw!'

but there's nothing I can fake... I am who I am. I am not a scholar, and I will never pretend to be. I think I am a good teacher, I try to inspire and I think I accomplish it at points. Getting students to do things and helping them in their lives. But I am not something beyond that and I've never said otherwise. In the beginning, when I was making presentations, so many time I was introduced as grandmaster Bruce Pandolfini, it would be embarrassing to have to say I am not a grandmaster. I must have done that hundreds of times: I am not a grandmaster.'

Winter also pointed out chess errors in Walter Tevis's *The Queen's Gambit* and wondered what role Pandolfini, who was mentioned in the introduction of the book as chess advisor, had played.

'In 1982, Random House called me to read his manuscript. And I did, and thereafter I met with him and his editor at the Random House office in New York. I told them I liked the story, but I thought it needed a lot of chessic work, and Walter didn't like that. I don't think he changed much in the book. He was a chess player

and he didn't want me to also interfere with his writing. He was an artist. That's understandable. I had very little input.

'But I did give him the title. As the meeting was coming to an end, and not going anywhere, and I was literally walking out of the door of the office – Walter simply didn't want to hire me and pay me – I said, your title is wrong. It should be *The Queen's Gambit*. I'm not sure why I said that, but I thought I had to tell them that. And the editor said, wait a second, come back, let's talk some more. And after a half an hour's discussion I was hired and Walter's consultant.

'I followed the entire shoot via Zoom. Messi was in Paris, Ronaldo in Manchester and I had to get up at 3 am'

Maybe they agreed to pick up the tab, I don't know, but that's how I got involved.'

Although he liked the book, Pandolfini could not have imagined that the Netflix series that was produced almost 40 years later would be such an incredible success. 'In 2018, Bill Horberg gave me a call. We had known each other from *Searching for Bobby Fischer*, because he was the producer on that as well. He said, Bruce, we are going to do it! I said, what are you going to do? We'll do *The Queen's Gambit*. It took off from there. With him and Scott Frank, Alan Scott. And I suggested Garry Kasparov. Ninety per cent was filmed in Berlin, 10 per cent or even less in Toronto, some of the technical things were done in New York and Los Angeles. And I had to be in Berlin for a lot of it. But there were others, the staff was quite good and helpful. Garry (Kasparov) was not on set, he provided a few of the positions and just to have him associated with the project is significant. One of the all-time greats. He also provided a lot of wonderful background, information on Russian and Soviet chess, the culture and what have you. It was a team effort. I had to train the actors. I had to initially create the 92 chess positions that were needed. There were actually more than 350 positions generated for the series. Most of them you don't see because they were off camera, but to create a certain legitimacy to the ambiance the players handled real chess positions as much as possible. It was fun.

'Anya Taylor-Joy really got into the part. She's a very gifted individual, very talented and I have no doubt she would have been a decent chess player if she had learned it earlier on. But you don't have to be a good player to look like a good player obviously. That's the most important thing; that you look like you're really playing chess. So you have to be natural. How

Bruce Pandolfini with writer/producer Scott Frank, who first had tried to make *The Queen's Gambit* as a film before he pitched the idea of a miniseries to Netflix.

you grab the pieces is essential. If you look rather awkward there, you know that person is not a chess player.'

Engine proof of a perpetual
Such considerations didn't play a role when Pandolfini was hired as chess advisor at the end of last year for the Louis Vuitton photo shoot of Lionel Messi and Cristiano Ronaldo playing chess that broke the internet. The football stars only had to be at the chess board and were not required to play. Which doesn't mean that there are no untold stories about the shoot. Quite soon the chess world discovered that the position in the photo was from a game between Magnus Carlsen and Hikaru Nakamura that ended in a perpetual. And we also learned that Messi and Ronaldo didn't actually meet but were photographed in different locations. But Pandolfini can add some more behind-the-scenes news and gossip. 'The interesting thing was that their representatives wanted to make very sure that neither won. So I gave a position with perpetual check, there was no doubt it was a draw. But they wanted analytic proof! And so I had

to provide Stockfish's and Fritz's evaluation that the game was a draw!'

'I followed the entire shoot via Zoom. Messi was in Paris, Ronaldo in Manchester and I had to get up at 3 am. The players barely spoke, just some meaningless words. I doubt that they play chess at all.'

Looking at his fascinating career it doesn't seem far-fetched to see Bruce Pandolfini as one of the most successful coaches of all time. Yet, he is rarely if ever compared to the top coaches that have held centre stage in professional chess in the past decades. The Soviet coaches and the

> 'I have sat with two people over a chess board who were out of this world. One was Bobby Fischer, the other was Garry Kasparov'

Indian coaches now, who hoped and hope to bring us future champions. Pandolfini sees a clear difference himself as well, between the teacher that he feels he is, and the coaches who put great emphasis on professionalism and hard work. 'These coaches are great, the top coaches around the world. I think they focus more on the material that they are presenting. I do that too, but I also do other stuff. Once I understand the student, I inundate them with material that is relevant for who they are. Look at all the classic examples. I like to go through chess history a lot, show the ideas of Anderssen, Morphy, Steinitz and go all the way up to Carlsen and all today's great players. I draw so much from Alekhine, Botvinnik, their commentary. I doubt that Alekhine saw everything he said he did, but it doesn't matter, they are great examples, right? And Botvinnik. I met him several times and once I interviewed him at Carnegie Mellon. In a way he was one of the greatest chess teachers of all time. Certainly one of them. So many people have learned from his ideas and his approach to chess study and his preparation.'

He also speaks highly of Mark Dvoretsky ('the greatest trainer; there is no one like him') and fondly remembers their meetings and how they once successfully analysed a rook ending of Josh Waitzkin together. Continuing about players whose ideas determined the course of chess history he calls Magnus Carlsen 'quite possibly the greatest player of all time', but quickly adds that the same argument can be made for Bobby Fischer and Garry Kasparov. 'I have sat with two people over a chess board who were out of this world. One was Bobby Fischer, the other was Garry Kasparov. You could see they were just on another plane. I wouldn't know why Bobby Fischer wouldn't be up there now. The guy was a genius, why wouldn't he be a genius now?' ∎

MAXIMize your Tactics

with Maxim Notkin

Find the best move in the positions below

Solutions on page 91

1. Black to play

2. Black to play

3. White to play

4. Black to play

5. Black to play

6. White to play

7. White to play

8. Black to play

9. White to play

Judit Polgar

Hall of Fame

The World Chess Hall of Fame in St. Louis is rightly famous for both their wonderful chess exhibitions and the tributes they pay to the greats of our game. The latest inductees were Miguel Najdorf (1910-1997), Eugenio Torre and Judit Polgar. A huge honour, our columnist writes, and a perfect reason to finally visit St. Louis, where she bumped into chess players on practically every corner.

Fate had it that for many years I did not have the occasion to visit the World Chess Hall of Fame, until recent events made my visit inevitable. Founded in 1986 by the then USCF President Steven Doyle, the World Chess Hall of Fame was originally known as the U.S. Chess Hall of Fame. In 2001, a new list was created, which included the world's most outstanding players. The first inductees were Robert Fischer, Jose Raul Capablanca, Emanuel Lasker, Paul Morphy and Wilhelm Steinitz. It should be mentioned that Fischer and Morphy were also part of the first 'wave of induction' into the U.S. Chess Hall of Fame in 1986.

The WCHOF is a non-profit institution and has been located in St. Louis since 2011, across the street from the St. Louis Chess Club. It presents world-class exhibitions that explore the connection between chess and art, culture and history. The institution also puts strong emphasis on Chess in Schools. As a curiosity, the world's largest chess piece can be seen in front of the entrance.

I must confess that I have been partly 'responsible' myself for not visiting the World Chess Hall of Fame in the past. In 2011, I was invited to play in St. Louis, but things changed after I qualified for the World Cup and advanced all the way to the quarter finals, after eliminating Karjakin and Dominguez, among others. Since the final part of the World Cup clashed with the event in St. Louis, I had to cancel my participation in the latter.

It was a huge honour for me to be inducted as a member together with Miguel Najdorf and Eugenio Torre in 2021. Due to the pandemic, the in-person induction had to be postponed till 2022. I was excited and was looking forward to finally visit the Hall of Fame. It was wonderful to see all kinds of memorabilia about Bobby and his historical 1972 match against Spassky: videos, pictures, cartoons, posters, handwritten documents, a replica of the chess table, the chairs and many more historical items that would make the heart of any collector beat faster.

The induction of Eugenio Torre had been made prior to my visit, during the opening ceremony of the 2022 U.S. Championship. I could not make it that day and my induction took place at the annual gala at the end of the year, with hundreds of guests, including world-class players, politicians, business leaders and many others who appreciate the work of Rex Sinquefield and his wife Jeanne Cairns.

'I am not used to meeting with several top players at the same day and place, if there is no chess tournament going on!'

At the end of the year gala Strategy Across the Board, Judit Polgar was interviewed by journalist and influencer Sharon Carpenter.

It is not by chance that chess is flourishing in St. Louis. Besides several world top grandmasters moving there from all over the world, many other players are joining the local chess community as a part of the club's efforts to spread chess in St. Louis at all levels. Add to that a rich university chess life, with many grandmasters playing for very strong teams, I feel that it is no exaggeration to say that St. Louis is the World Capital of Chess!

Bumping into a chess player on practically every corner of the city was a pleasantly surprising experience. Before leaving for the airport, I had an enjoyable conversation with Fabiano Caruana and Cristian Chirila for their C-Squared podcast. After that, I went together with Fabi and Tatev Abrahamyan to a cafeteria where, purely by chance, Aronian showed up together with his family! I am not used to meeting with several top players at the same day and place if there is no chess tournament going on!

When I look back on my career, there is one game from my teenage years that I particularly remember. Trusting yourself is essential, of course, but occasional doubts about your real strength are inevitable. Therefore, the experts' recognition is an important element, too. I remember that after I had won against Uhlmann in 1990, at the age of 14, Jan Timman said in an interview that this was *the* game that made him realize that I was exceptionally talented. Other voices subscribed to this point of view, too, and Korchnoi's later statement that I was a coffee house player only added some spice to the issue.

Polgar – Uhlmann
OHRA-B Amsterdam 1990
position after 16...♕f6

A former world title Candidate, Wolfgang Uhlmann was an outstanding French Defence expert. He never hesitated to go for sharp and even dangerous positions. Without undue modesty, I can be proud of my attacking vision, quite characteristic for my style, which proved to be more accurate than Uhlmann's defensive skills and sense of danger.

17.♘e5!?
After concentrating all my pieces on the kingside, this knight jump looks natural, since it allows f2-f4, including the rook on f1 into the attack.

17...cxd4?!

Uhlmann probably thought that before taking on e5, it was useful to exchange the central pawns, failing to anticipate my answer.

17...♘xe5! was necessary, even though it entails a pawn sacrifice. 18.dxe5 ♕g5! 19.♕xg5 hxg5 20.♖e3.

We both considered this to be good for me, since the pawn on g5 is doomed, but Black can get adequate compensation. 20...♖f4 21.♖g3 ♖a4 22.♖a1 ♗d7 23.♖xg5 b5 I do not have enough resources for continuing my attack, while Black has strong queen-side counterplay.

18.f4!

This strong move sacrifices two pawns, for the sake of including my king's rook into the attack. The exchange on e5 would allow me to open the f-file, with decisive effect, so Uhlmann did not find anything better than completing the pawn grabbing.

18...dxc3

19.g4!?

Advancing the g-pawn used to be one of my trademarks. It is a good idea here, but 19.♗d3!, followed by g4-g5

would have been even stronger. The point is that the black queen would be stuck on f6, due to the necessity of preventing ♕h5-g6.

19...♖e7

20.♗d3

Played according to the principle 'better late than never'!

However, 20.g5 ♘xe5 21.♖xe5 was very strong, too.

20...♕e8

Preventing ♕g6.

21.♘g6

I did not have the least intention of capturing on f8, of course. The only purpose of my last move was to maintain my queen in an attacking position.

21...♗d7

A desperate attempt to catch up in development.

22.g5!

With all my pieces optimally placed, the attack develops as naturally as a child's smile, as Fischer once wrote.

22...♖f7 23.gxh6 gxh6 24.♔h1! ♘e7 25.♖g1 ♘f5

'Apart from being a player with a glorious career, Najdorf was one of the most colourful persons I have ever met'

26.♘e7+

Since this wins material, I thought that my opponent would resign at once.

The game would have ended sooner after 26.♗xf5 ♖xf5 27.♕xh6 ♔f7 28.♕h7+ ♔f6 29.♘e5, mating soon.

26...♔f8 27.♘xf5 ♖f6 28.♕g4 ♕f7 29.♘d6 ♖xf4 30.♘xf7

Good enough, but not the best.

I missed another shortcut to the win: 30.♖ef1! e5 31.♖xf4 exf4 32.h4, with a decisive attack.

30...♖xg4 31.♖xg4 ♔xf7

I have a decisive material advantage, but due to his strong pawn chain, Uhlmann could hang on for more than 20 moves before resigning (1-0, 53).

Despite my slight inaccuracies after the main job had been done, I am pleased by the way I built up and developed my attack after Uhlmann's careless capture on d4.

I fulfilled my final GM norm in December 1991 and was awarded the title in 1992. This way, I beat Fischer's long-lasting record by becoming a grandmaster at an age a few weeks younger than him.

The whole year of 1992 was special for me. I started receiving good invitations to top-level tournaments as the youngest grandmaster of the moment and I had the opportunity to meet with many legendary players. Among others, I had the pleasure of being acquainted with Najdorf and Torre, who, as mentioned above, were inducted into the Hall of Fame in the same year as me. Najdorf, or Don Miguel as friends and fans call him, does not need any special recommendations. Apart from being a player with a glorious career, he was one of the most colourful persons I have ever met. I have participated in several events organized by him in Buenos Aires. After he regrettably passed away, I also played at his Memorial.

I vividly remember an amusing incident from 1992, when I played in the Argentinian capital for the first time. Don Miguel's attention was captured by Ivan Morovic's position (in his game against Nikolic, if I remember correctly). When Morovic stood up for a short walk while his opponent was thinking, Najdorf sat on his chair in order to examine the position better. The situation turned amusing when Ivan returned after his opponent had replied, in order to think over his next move, but Don Miguel did not seem to see anything bar the position, and surely did not notice him. Morovic had to come up with a long and polite sentence, asking the living legend to allow him to continue his game.

1992 was also the year of the politically controversial return match Fischer-Spassky. My family met

By coincidence, we can also point at a game that promoted the young Fischer as a huge promise to the public opinion, the same way the win over Uhlmann worked for me. Aged 13, he produced what later was called 'The Game of the Century'.

Donald Byrne – Bobby Fischer
New York 1956
position after 11.♗g5

The character of the game differs from that of my game against the German legend. It introduces Fischer as a player with excellent tactical skills and a good feel for dynamics. The game is widely known, so I will only show a short fragment, without detailed comments.

11...♘a4!!

'Legends may not notice that they are sharing true treasures and secrets, as these seem just natural to them...'

Fischer a few months after that and my father's insistence that Budapest is beautiful and charming, with an exquisite cuisine eventually led to him to pay a short visit to our city... which resulted in him living there for years. Fischer enjoyed the city and Hungarian food, loved to visit the thermal baths, and was happy to frequently meet his old friends Pal Benko and Lajos Portisch.

The first combination, based on White's hanging pieces.

12.♕a3
12.♘xa4 ♘xe4, followed by ...♗xf3 and ...♘xg5, wins a pawn and gains a considerable positional advantage.
12...♘xc3 13.bxc3 ♘xe4 14.♗xe7 ♕b6 15.♗c4 ♘xc3!
The second tactical moment.
16.♗c5
16.♕xc3 runs into 16...♖fe8 17.♕e3

♗xf3 18.gxf3 ♕c7, with the same evaluation as above.
16...♖fe8+ 17.♔f1 ♗e6!

The third pseudo-sacrifice in a seven-move sequence.
18.♗xb6
18.♗xe6 ♕b5+ leads to a well-known version of smothered mate:
19.♔g1 ♘e2+ 20.♔f1 ♘g3+ 21.♔g1 ♕f1+ 22.♖xf1 ♘e2, mate.
18...♗xc4+ 19.♔g1 ♘e2+ 20.♔f1 ♘xd4+ 21.♔g1 ♘e2+ 22.♔f1 ♘c3+ 23.♔g1 axb6 24.♕b4 ♖a4 25.♕xb6 ♘xd1
Black's combination has worked in amazingly, and his material advantage is decisive now. Fischer won on move 41.

As he was a good friend of Bobby's, Eugenio Torre visited him in Budapest, on which occasion I met him personally. One of Torre's most outstanding achievements is his participation in 22 Olympiads between 1970 and 2014, a span of 44 years. He only missed the Olympiad in 2008.

My induction into the World Chess Hall of Fame was an extraordinary experience, but it also gave me the opportunity to make an incursion into the past, remembering the moments I met some big legends of chess. On such occasions, one can learn simply by watching them play, but also by observing the way they talk, assess positions, tell stories and comment on life experiences. Many of them may not notice that they are sharing true treasures and secrets, as these seem just natural to them... ■

Thomas Willemze

Club players, test your decision-making skills!

What would you play?

Long-range pieces clearly thrive in open positions. What other factors strengthen their potential?

Chess can be played at various speeds. Cautious players prefer closed positions with carefully prepared pawn breaks and slow knight manoeuvres. Thrill-seekers strive for open positions in which long-range pieces can reach their full potential.

Eva-Maria Schmied (1718) and Simon Lang (1942) clearly belonged to the second category in their game in the 2022 Ceske Budejovice Open. An early trade of all knights and a couple of pawns led to a fascinating battle with an abundance of open files, ranks, and diagonals. Fasten your seatbelts. You are about to experience the dynamics of the long-range pieces yourself.

I hope you enjoy these exercises and will be able to make your long-range pieces happy. You can find the full analysis of this game on the pages below.

Exercise 1

position after 21....♗xc3

Black has just removed the last knight from the board to give the floor to the long-range pieces. It is your turn now. Would you duly recapture the bishop with 22.bxc3, or can you find a more promising continuation instead?

Exercise 2

position after 34...♖c4

Black is under severe pressure in this position. Can you come up with a way for White to exploit his opponent's poorly coordinated pieces?

Exercise 3

position after 36.♕b3

In this complex position, Black has only one move that will put him into the driver's seat. What should he do? Should he clear the back rank with 36...♔a7, open the long diagonal with 36...e4, or threaten to win the queen with 36...♖4c5 ?

Exercise 4

position after 38.♗d3

Black is winning. What would you play? Pick up a pawn with 38...♖xc3, open up the long diagonal with 38...e4, or trade rooks with 38...♗f7 ?

Eva-Maria Schmied (1718)
Simon Lang (1942)
Ceske Budejovice 2022
Sicilian Defence, Keres Attack

1.e4 c5 2.♘f3 d6 3.d4 cxd4 4.♘xd4 ♘f6 5.♘c3 e6 6.h3 a6

7.g4 This aggressive move prepares the fianchetto of White's light-squared bishop and intends to meet the typical d5-break with g4-g5 to chase the supporting knight away.

7...h6 8.♗e3 ♘c6 9.♗g2 ♘e5

10.♕e2 White clears the back rank for queenside castling and prevents the annoying 10...♘c4.

10...g5! It is very important for Black to maintain his knight on e5

'Opening up the kingside looks tempting, but also provides the enemy pieces with more breathing space'

and prevent his opponent from grabbing too much space with the upcoming f2-f4.

11.f4 gxf4 12.♗xf4 ♕c7

13.0-0-0 Black does not mind the doubled pawns arising after 13.♗xe5. On the contrary! 13...dxe5 would give him a firm grip on the centre and leave White with highly vulnerable dark squares due to the absence of her bishop.

13...♗d7 14.♖hf1 ♗e7

15.g5 Opening up the kingside looks tempting, but also gives the enemy pieces more elbow room. The most common move in this position is 15.♘f3, to add pressure on the black knight.

15...hxg5 16.♗xg5

16...♘d5 There is nothing wrong with trading the dark-squared bishops, but

Black should be very careful not to release the blocked e4-pawn. 16...♘g8 was the required move, with equal chances for both players after 17.♗d2 b5 18.a3 ♖b8.

17.exd5! After this move, White can safely trade her dark-squared bishop, since she will soon shift her attention to the light squares.

17...♗xg5+ 18.♔b1 0-0-0

19.♘f3! This simple and strong move prepares a knight trade to increase White's influence in the centre. Stockfish suggests an even stronger exchange sacrifice, which would have given her total control over the light squares: 19.♖xf7! ♘xf7 20.dxe6 ♘e5 21.exd7+ ♕xd7 22.♘b3.

ANALYSIS DIAGRAM

An exchange is a very small price for such an overwhelming initiative. With ♘a5 and ♘d5 in the air, this position is a text-book example of opposite-coloured bishops favouring the attacker!

19...♗f6 This move causes the collapse of Black's centre. It was essential to keep the long diagonal closed with 19...♘xf3 20.♖xf3 ♔b8 21.♖xf7 e5. White is a healthy pawn

up, but there is still a lot to play for.
20.♞xe5 ♝xe5 21.♖xf7 ♝xc3

The knights are gone. From now on, the fight will about controlling files, ranks and diagonals.

22.bxc3 This move was not the right answer to **Exercise 1**, as you may have concluded from the way the question was formulated. Black is threatening to close the centre, which means that we needed a more forceful continuation. 22.dxe6!, to open the long diagonal, was the way to go! White crashes through after 22...♝c5

ANALYSIS DIAGRAM

23.♖d3!. White will soon regain the piece with exd7, after which the serious ♖d3-b3 threat remains.

22.♖d3 ♝e5 23.dxe6 leads to the same position and hence was equally strong.
22...e5! This move levels the game. Black will be relieved that the long diagonal will stay closed for the moment.
23.♕e3

23...♖h4 The rook is about to swing from h8 to a4 in two moves! This elegant rook lift is a clear example of the increased opportunities for long-range pieces when you remove the knights and a couple of pawns from the board.
24.♖df1 ♖a4 25.♖f8

White is eager to highlight the drawback of the Black rook's trip to a4. She wants to trade one rook to bring the

other one to the back rank to attack the enemy king.
25.♕a7 would be a very unfortunate way to attack the king, because 25...♕xc3! would decide the game at once. White is defenceless against the 26...♖b4-threat, and 26.♕a8+ would only jeopardize the white queen after 26...♔c7.
25...♝e8

It is tempting to block the back rank, but this move opens up the 7th rank instead! The cool 25...♔b8! would have kept the game level.
26.♔b2

This is too slow. White has missed a nice opportunity to grab the initiative with 26.♕a7!. Now, 26...♕xc3 will be refuted by 27.♕a8+ ♔c7.

ANALYSIS DIAGRAM

28.♖1f7+! ♔b6 29.♖xb7+! ♔c5 30.♕a7+ ♔c4 31.♖c7+, winning the queen and the game.

26...♕a5 27.♖a1 ♔b8 28.♗f3

White is suddenly very passive and must allow a series of checks.

28...♕b5+ 29.♔c1 ♕f1+ 30.♔b2 ♕b5+ 31.♔c1 ♕f1+ 32.♔b2

32...♕xh3

We should thank Black for his brave attempt to keep the game going, because otherwise the thrilling finale of this game would never have taken place.

33.♖h1 ♕d7 34.♕b6

34...♖c4

This move fails to relieve the pres-

sure from the black pieces. 34...♕c7! was called for, with a level game after 35.♕xc7+ ♔xc7 36.♖hh8 ♖f4!.

35.♖hh8

This logical moves keeps Black in the game. The correct answer to **Exercise 2** was to lure away the defender of the black rook with 35.♖h7!. 35...♕c8 will now run into 36.♖hh8 (threatening ♕xd8!), while 35...♕xh7 is just as bad on account of 36.♕xd8+ ♖c8 37.♕xd6+.

35...♖dc8 36.♕b3

Too passive. The queen was already well-placed, and White should have gone for complications with 36.♗e2!.

36...♖4c5

36...♔a7! was the only path to an advantage. The key to **Exercise 3** was that Black can meet 37.♖xe8 ♖xe8 38.♖xe8 with the powerful intermediate move 38...♖c5!. White is in serious trouble, since she must choose between surrendering her rook, or allowing 39...♖b5.

36...e4 would not yield much, because

'Long-range pieces flourish when you remove the knights and a couple of pawns from the board'

White has the simplifying 37.♗g4 ♕xg4 38.♖xe8, with a level game.

37.♗e2 ♔a7 38.♗d3

This move provokes Black to finish the game at once. 38.c4! would have maintained the balance.

38...e4!

Well done! Black found the right answer to **Exercise 4**! A pawn is a small price for an open diagonal. Black is on his way to direct his queen to the long diagonal to decide the game.

38...♗f7 would give White a slightly more pleasant position after 39.♖xc8 ♖xc8 40.♖h7!.

38...♖xc3 is not as convincing as the game move, but does give Black ample compensation for the exchange after 39.♕b4 ♖xd3! 40.cxd3 ♕c7!.

39.♗f1 ♕g7!

This was the point! It is game over.

40.♖xe8 ♖xc3 41.♖xc8 ♖xc8+

White resigned.

Conclusion

This game has taught us that long-range pieces flourish when you remove the knights and a couple of pawns from the board. Black won this exciting game because he kept a cooler head in the complications. ■

1. Salinas-Caruana
Titled Tuesday 2022

41...♖xg4! Eliminating the bishop Black provides access to the d1-square for his rook. **42.♖xg4 ♖d1+ 43.♔h2 ♕h1+ 44.♔g3 ♖g1** Mate.

2. Coenen-Lamby
Bundesliga 2022

The white king is 'good' and the black bishop 'bad'. Two pawn moves turn the tables. **57...f4+! 58.♔xf4 e5+!** 0-1 (59.dxe5 ♖g4 mate).

3. Makarian-Kamsky
Titled Tuesday 2022

35.♖xa5! Black resigned in view of 35...♖xd7 36.♖xa8+ or 35...♖xa5 36.♕d8+. And 35...♕xa5 36.bxa5 ♖xb1+ 37.♗xb1.

4. Fruchard-Shchekachev
Paris 2022

50...♖g4! Now 51.♗e3 ♖g3 loses the queen. **51.fxg4 ♘xg4+** And the queen is lost anyway, as the king's moves lead to a back rank mate. **52.♕xg4 fxg4 53.♗e3 h3** White resigned.

5. Rustemov-Tokman
Titled Tuesday 2022

It's all about the a7-g1 diagonal! **27...♕b8! 28.♖c6** The white bishop still protects the diagonal, but... **28...♕xb6+! 29.♖xb6 ♗d4+ 30.♔h1 ♖f1** Mate.

6. Mazé-Harff
Bundesliga 2022

The f7-pawn is heavily defended, but what about f8? **27.♖xg6+! fxg6 28.♘xh5+! ♔h7** (28...gxh5 29.♕f8+ ♔h7 30.♕h6+ ♔g8 31.♖f8 and mate) **29.♘f6+ ♔h8 30.♘xd7** Black resigned.

7. Ya.Quesada-Holm
Benasque 2022

24.♘f7! Much more effective than 24.♖h8+ ♔xh8 25.♘f7+ ♔g7 26.♘xe5 ♘xe5. **24...♔xf7 25.♖h7+ ♔e6** If 25...♔g8, 26.♕h6 mating. **26.♖e1** Now the queen is lost. Black resigned on move 37.

8. Dobrowolski-Donchenko
Pardubice rapid 2022

19...♘d4 20.♕a4 The queen had a very limited choice. **20...♘e2+ 21.♔h1** The king had no choice at all. **21...♖h3!** White resigned since 22.gxh3 ♕f3 is mate while otherwise there is no defence against 22...♖xh2+! 23.♔xh2 ♕h5 mating.

9. Alekseenko-Bewersdorff
Biel 2022

33.♖xh6+! gxh6 34.♖xh6+ ♔g8 The white queen joins with great force. 34...♔g7 fails to 35.♕g3+! ♔xh6 36.♕g6 mate, and 34...♖h7 35.♖xh7+ ♔xh7 36.♘xf6+ loses the queen. **35.♕g3+ ♖g7 36.♕h4** Mate is inevitable, Black resigned.

Revisiting history

An awful lot has been written about the history of our game, but what do we really know? Matthew Sadler read two new books that closely examine the development of chess ideas in the 18th and 19th century, challenging many a commonly held view. 'Both fantastic books that should definitely land on your must-read lists!

Thinking back to my earliest experiences in junior chess, I realise how much of my success at the time was due to opening theory. Not in the sense that I knew a lot, but the little I knew was powerful enough to give me a series of easy wins at the under-9 level.

I'll mention in particular this trick in the Morra Gambit:

1.e4 c5 2.d4 cxd4 3.c3 dxc3 4.♘xc3 ♘c6 5.♘f3 d6 6.♗c4 ♘f6

7.e5 dxe5 8.♕xd8+ ♘xd8 9.♘b5 ♔d7 10.♘xe5+ ♔e8 11.♘c7 Mate.

Obviously, I had decent natural chess skills too – in particular, I applied the technique of winning won positions by exchanging pieces to reach a winning endgame very effectively – but the bedrock of my success was knowing more than my opponents right from the opening.

I still vividly remember the moment of revelation I experienced however when I faced an opponent who managed to navigate safely past the opening phase without getting mated: 'But... I'm a pawn down!' That led to a counter-reaction during which I tried first the English Opening (not really me) and then the London System.

My London System knowledge was minimal, but again based around the knowledge of one unpleasant attacking structure:

1.d4 d5 2.♘f3 ♘f6 3.♗f4 e6 4.e3

♗e7 5.♘bd2 c5 6.c3 ♘c6 7.♗d3 0-0 8.♘e5 ♘xe5 9.dxe5

This was the key idea I'd been shown. Capturing on e5 with the d-pawn gives White a typical attacking structure and games often continued:

9...♘d7 10.♕h5 f5 11.g4

With a very dangerous initiative, and I beat my first 2200-player in this way. Around the age of 12, I suddenly decided that I was going to get seriously into opening theory. As far as I remember, it was completely my own decision and I went at it like a maniac, without telling anyone. I remember the uncomfortable and disconnected sense of having landed somewhere in the middle of a timeline, obviously unsure where this path would lead you but also rather blank as to what had brought you here!

For example, influenced by some commentaries on a game of Kasparov's, I became obsessed by a line of the Four Pawns Attack against the King's Indian:

1.d4 ♘f6 2.c4 g6 3.♘c3 ♗g7 4.e4 d6 5.f4 0-0 6.♘f3 c5 7.d5 e6 8.♗e2 exd5 9.e5

Learning resources were scarce (no engines, no databases!) and none of the books I had helped me (just 12 at the time) understand why people had made the choices they had (even for example 6...c5 and 7...e6) or how they had worked out that these were the best moves. It really made you feel as if you had arrived way too late to the party to ever get involved!

I guess that we are talking about the significant value of experience back in those pre-computer days. If you'd been playing for 20 or 30 years, you might have seen the variation developing and you would have some idea about the reasons for the current state of theory, but a junior had no chance of knowing any of that. It's one of the joys of opening preparation nowadays that any player – young or old – can find out fairly effortlessly who was the first person to try it and (thanks to elite games, opening surveys and engines) understand why a modern line developed as it did. However, older lines often remain as murky as ever.

This long introduction is an attempt to explain why *Chess Theory from Stamma to Steinitz, 1735-1894* by Frank Hoffmeister (McFarland) appealed to me so much. The author traces the development of chess theoretical knowledge in all phases of the game (opening, middlegame and endgame) through the books published and the games played by leading players during that period.

I've always been a keen reader of books by – and about – players of bygone eras, and the names of some of the books examined by Hoffmeister were familiar to me (*Bilguer's Handbuch*, for example) but usually in a derogatory context ('*Bilguer's Handbuch* recommended move "y", but great player "x" knew much better'). I knew nothing about the

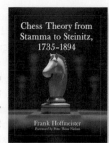

**Chess Theory from Stamma to Steinitz
Frank Hoffmeister
McFarland, 2022**
★★★★★

content of such books, how they came to exist, the sources and expertise they drew on and the quality of the judgements made. Hoffmeister does an amazing job both in providing the historical context (it seems that *Bilguer's Handbuch* was started by Bilguer but completed after his death by the strong player Von der Lasa) and also in summarising the highlights of these manuals, many of which are 300 pages or more long!

I think I can safely say that I've never learnt so much from a chess book! With limited space, I'll list just a few things that struck me the most.

I was definitely appalled at how little attention was paid to 1.d4 and 1.♘f3 for most of the 18th and 19th centuries. Of course I understand that most attention would be fixed on 1.e4, but it's shocking to see 1.d4 d5 2.c4 e6 3.♘c3 ♘f6 4.e3 still being considered as the main line against the Queen's Gambit Declined late in the 19th century, or Zukertort's 1.♘f3 being described as a novelty by Steinitz in 1880! It's especially the contrast between the often impressive ingenuity displayed by authors in the analysis of King's Gambit lines, and the palpable lack of enthusiasm for queen's pawn openings that strikes you.

There are also many moments that look like huge jumps in knowledge where you can only wonder to yourself how these analysts came

upon the ideas or even entertained the thought that those ideas might be viable. For example, in Jaenisch's deeply impressive *Nouvelle Analyse* from 1842, Jaenisch recommends meeting

1.e4 e5 2.♘f3 ♘c6 3.♗c4 ♘f6 4.♘g5 d5 5.exd5 with 5...♘a5

...instead of the always played 5...♘xd5 (for which Von der Lasa provided a very interesting piece of analysis in 1843!). It's always seemed such an odd line for Black to me – pawn down, knight on the rim and a broken structure – so it's very impressive to see an analyst in 1842 stepping past this ugliness and focusing on Black's dynamic compensation.

Jaenisch also provides a first and impressive analysis of Petroff's Defence identifying all of the main attempts for White and Black (in both 3.♘xe5 and 3.d4) and providing plausible and modern-looking continuations in all of them as well as some fairly sophisticated and subtle evaluations.

Hoffmeister points out however that the book's influence was limited, as it was written in French (which made it inaccessible to German readers) but used the German algebraic form of notation (to which French readers were not accustomed)! It seems that this work was also widely ignored in Russia.

It's quite bizarre to see the general attitude to the French Defence: always denigrated as an inferior defence and yet for the most part never analysed beyond the dull Exchange Variation (3.exd5). The first to take the alternatives 3.♘c3 and 3.♘d2 seriously were

Hoffmeister does an amazing job both in providing the historical context and also in summarising the highlights of these manuals

the English amateurs Freeborough and Ranken, who, in their excellent *Chess Openings Ancient and Modern* from 1896, suggested the possible continuations 3...♘f6 4.e5 ♘fd7 5.♗d3 c5 6.c3 ♘c6 7.♘e2 ♕b6 8.♘f3 f6 9.exf6 ♘xf6 and 3...c5 4.dxc5 ♗xc5 5.exd5 exd5 or 5...♕xd5 as equal.

The Caro-Kann was 'cancelled' even more thoroughly until Horatio Caro published an article in the late 1880s in a German chess magazine. With the exception of Caro's strange recommendation of meeting the Exchange Caro-Kann with 3...♕xd5 (1.e4 c6 2.d4 d5 3.exd5 ♕xd5), the analysis makes a solid, modern impression with Caro considering both modern main lines 3.♘c3 dxe4 4.♘xe4 ♗f5 and 4...♘f6, as well as 3.e5 ♗f5.

The Sicilian received wildly varying evaluations throughout the 18th and 19th centuries without being analysed that much! Once again Freeborough and Ranken had a pretty ground-breaking role (highlighted by Peter Heine Nielsen in his foreword) with their analysis of this line:

1.e4 c5 2.♘c3 ♘c6 3.♘f3 e6 4.d4 cxd4 5.♘xd4 ♘f6 6.♘xc6 bxc6 7.e5 ♘d5 8.♘e4

and their suggestion of **8...♕c7 9.f4 ♕b6**, which is still fertile ground for investigation nowadays!

I wasn't too surprised that endgames received fairly scarce attention from books in the 18th and 19th century apart from Berger's *Theorie und Praxis der Endspiele* – a book

Emanuel Lasker confessed to taking to all of his tournaments. However, it was shocking to see how scarce concrete middlegame advice was during this period – including Steinitz's books. Actually, many of the general insights attributed to Steinitz might also be ascribed to the Italian writers Ponziani and Del Rio at the beginning of the 19th century. For example, in 1820 Ponziani advised 'Whoever has the advantage of the attack is in a state to give law to the enemy; therefore all means must be used to obtain and preserve it, menacing and annoying the enemy constantly, to gain advantage from any irregularity in his answers', which sounds a lot like Steinitz.

'When a sufficient advantage has been obtained, a player must attack or the advantage will be dissipated.' Del Rio's advice from 1802 (alas left unpublished until 1984!) is also very interesting: 'It is very important to guard against certain small disadvantages, which bring others along with them. This piece shut off, castling forfeited, that Knight still not moved out, that enemy pawn allowed to move too far, may worsen the position, demand reinforcements on the other side, and little by little turn the battle into a rout. For want of a nail the shoe was lost, for want of a shoe the horse was lost.' This is reminiscent of Steinitz's famous phrase 'accumulation of small advantages' (which, as Hoffmeister points out, was hidden away in Steinitz's obituary for John Cochrane).

■ ■ ■

The role and influence of Steinitz is very interesting and forms a major part both of this book and the book I read as a companion to it: Willy Hendriks' superb *The Ink War* (New In Chess). It was lovely to read these two books together, as many of the same characters appear in both, which gives a wonderful sense of recognition!

Hendriks' book examines the competitive rivalry between Wilhelm (later also William) Steinitz and Johannes Zukertort in the 1870s and

The Ink War
Willy Hendriks
New In Chess, 2022
★★★★★

1880s with their 1886 World Championship Match as the fulcrum, examining in particular Steinitz' characterisation of their struggle as that of Modernity against Romanticism (with Steinitz on the side of Modernity of course!).

From my point of view, I've come to view Steinitz through the prism of a comment I once heard Garry Kasparov make about his eternal rival Anatoly Karpov while fielding questions from members of the Clichy chess club for whom I played. At one stage Garry said 'Do you know when Karpov played his best chess? When he was losing to me!' The implication was that Karpov needed a real challenge to force him to display all of his talents, and that challenge could only be given by Garry. It's obviously a rather cheeky comment, and you can question it in Karpov's case, but when it comes to Steinitz, I might venture that Steinitz was stimulated to produce some of his deepest play in the first match he lost to Lasker and in his tournament play straight after that defeat. Before then, he was simply an extremely strong practical player with an iron will, a pronounced attacking bent and a belief in concrete play (evidenced by the odd opening variations he believed he could hold). In essence, his games are extremely strong for their time but still very much part of their time, and the openings he espoused during that period don't have much value in the modern age.

Hendriks' book takes us from London 1872 – the scene of Zukertort's first meeting with Steinitz – to the conclusion of their 1886 World

It was shocking to see how scarce concrete middlegame advice was during this period – including Steinitz's books

Championship match, taking in along the way the stormy disputes Steinitz and Zukertort fought out – many over analytical matters – through their respective British newspaper columns. Along the way we take in many different themes such as the lurking antipathy that the British chess scene harboured towards these dominant foreigners, as well as the deep-seated British tendency to venerate amateurism above professionalism. One episode that particularly resonated was Steinitz' passionate – desperate one might say – attempts to counter the expressed view that Morphy would easily defeat him (with pawn and move odds even!) if he were to return to chess. How could you explain how much chess had progressed in those 30 years since Morphy had last played a game and how antiquated his conception of the game would be? I wonder what Steinitz would think of the fact that 120 years later, some people are still asking whether Morphy could beat everyone if he returned!

Hendriks' comments to the chess games he examines are really good: just the right level of criticism tempered by generosity, acknowledging the excellence of certain decisions without being afraid to point out key mistakes. His annotations to the Steinitz-Zukertort 1886 World Championship match certainly brought it alive for me. In particular, I hadn't realised that Zukertort defended against Steinitz' Ruy Lopez with the Berlin and that Steinitz also struggled to make any headway! In the end, Steinitz switched from 1.e4 e5 2.♘f3

♘c6 3.♗b5 ♘f6 4.0-0 ♘xe4 5.♖e1 to 4.d3 (a setup favoured by Adolf Anderssen) and ended up scoring two wins in complicated middlegames, in which Zukertort definitely had his chances.

William Steinitz
Johannes Zukertort
World Championship match
United States 1886 (18)
Ruy Lopez, Berlin Variation

1.e4 e5 2.♘f3 ♘c6 3.♗b5 ♘f6 4.d3 d6
4...♗c5 is most played nowadays, but this is very reasonable too.
5.c3 g6 6.d4 ♗d7 7.♘bd2 ♗g7 8.dxe5 ♘xe5 9.♘xe5 dxe5 10.♕e2 0-0 11.f3 a5 12.♗d3 ♕e7 13.♘f1 ♗e6

The players had fought out this structure in Steinitz's previous white game and Zukertort improves his piece setup, putting the bishop to the natural e6-square rather than the passive c6-square he had previously chosen.
14.g4
Hendriks points out that if Zukertort had played like this and lost, then he would have been condemned for the 'romantic' chess which had been stamped out by Steinitz's 'modernity'. However, it was Steinitz playing White... 14.g4 certainly isn't without point and I could certainly imagine playing it myself. However, the engines are already clearly on Black's side. Black has holes to aim for and a lead in development to probe them!
14...♖fd8 15.h4 ♕d7
15...h5 is pointed out as a better option by Hendriks (allowing the knight

to retreat to d7 after g5), although I guess Zukertort may have feared the pawn sacrifice 16.♗g5 in reply.
16.♗c2 h5 17.g5
17.♗g5 hxg4 18.h5 ♘xh5 would be a natural human reaction to White's kingside pressure, sacrificing the exchange for a pawn, the two bishops and lots of dark squares. In any case, the King's Indian / Dragon Defence of ...h5 against a pawn storm of the g- and h-pawns was completely unknown to Zukertort, so this was an extremely good find over the board.
17...♘e8 18.♘e3

The commentators at the time were very much in favour of White's position, and I have a vague recollection of reading something about this position as a child and learning that White was much better! However, as Hendriks points out, the engines see little danger on the kingside and simply want to gain space on the queenside with ...a4, ...b5, ...c6 and ...♘d6, with a clear advantage for Black. However, according to contemporary accounts, Zukertort seemed under great strain by this stage of the match and drifted terribly, unable to put together a coherent plan for the rest of the game.
18...♕c6 19.c4 ♘d6 20.♗d3 ♖ab8 21.♘d5 ♗xd5 22.cxd5 ♕d7 23.♗d2 ♖a8 24.♖c1 c6 25.♖c5 cxd5 26.♖xd5 ♕a4 27.a3 b6 28.♗c3 ♕e8 29.♕f2 ♘c8 30.♗b5 ♕e7 31.♖xd8+ ♕xd8 32.0-0 ♘a7 33.♗c4 ♘c6 34.♗d5 ♖c8 35.f4 ♕d7 36.f5 ♘e7 37.♗a2 gxf5 38.exf5 ♗f8 39.♕f3 e4 40.♕xh5 1-0

All-in-all these are both fantastic books, shedding light and reason on a fascinating period of development in our game. Both should definitely land on your must-read lists! 5 stars to both!

■ ■ ■

I had a little less time for other books this month but I did have time for *The Exchange Sacrifice According to Tigran Petrosian* by Vassilios Kotronias. Kotronias annotates 36 games deeply, in which the great Armenian World Champion sacrifices the exchange (with another 88 games in unannotated form). Funnily enough, his most famous positional exchange sacrifice (against Reshevsky at the 1953 Candidates) is not one of them (it is presented in the introduction) but there is a lovely mix of the known (like the 1953 game against Troianescu, or 30...♖c4!! from the 1969 World Championship match against Spassky) and the unknown. Not all the sacrifices are successful or winning, some are for swindling, but all of them are very interesting.

Talking of the unknown, the very first game against Aleksandrov played in 1947 was new to me and is a nice illustration of the effort that Kotronias puts into his annotations and his books. I'm not sure I would normally have paid any attention to this game from Petrosian's youth but with Kotronias tempting you with spectacular variations, you can't help but be interested!

Tigran Petrosian
Aleksander Aleksandrov
Tbilisi 1947 (8)

position after 31...♕h6

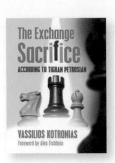

The Exchange Sacrifice According to Tigran Petrosian
Vassilios Kotronias
Russell Enterprises, 2022
★★★★☆

We join the game at move 32 with a complicated fight still ongoing. With such a firm barrier of pawns on e4 and f5 and some easy targets for White's pieces (such as g5 or the doubled c-pawns), you would intuitively expect White to be much better. Petrosian's choice (32.e5 – an exchange sacrifice of course!) was quite a holey choice and gave Black unexpected counterplay chances. Kotronias analyses a very interesting alternative.

32.e5
32.♖g1 (now that's a way to sacrifice the exchange!) 32...♕h4 33.♖f4 (33.♖xg5+ ♔g7 34.♖xg7+ ♔xg7 35.♖f3 ♗e5, stopping ♖g3, gives Black reasonable hopes of saving the game despite the two-pawn deficit) 33...♕h6 34.♖g3 ♗xc3 35.bxc3 ♖b1 36.♕d2 ♖7b2 37.♕xb2 ♖xb2 38.♗xb2. I'm not sure I'd really know whether White was winning or losing from afar: that back rank looks pretty airy. However, Kotronias goes further and shows that Black can add remarkably little to the existing pressure: 38...♕h5 39.c4 ♕d1+ 40.♖g1 ♕xd3 41.♖xg5+ ♔f7 42.♗e5

ANALYSIS DIAGRAM

Everything is protected now and the f-pawn will decide!
32...♗xf2
32...♕h4 was even stronger, according to Kotronias, with the lovely follow-up 33.♖g2 ♗xg2+ 34.♔xg2 h5. This gives the black king some room (...h7/h6) to escape from checks while taking away the escape square g4 from the white king. A typical line is now 35.e6 ♖xb2 36.♗xb2 ♖xb2 37.♕xb2 ♕xe1 38.♕b8+ ♔h7 39.♕c7+ ♔h6 and Black will mate though it's still not completely obvious! 40.♕g3 ♕g1+ 41.♔f3 ♕f1+ 42.♔e4 ♕h1+ 43.♕f3 ♕xh2 with ...♕e5+ to follow.
33.♕xf2 ♖g4

Kotronias annotates 36 games deeply, in which the great Armenian World Champion sacrifices the exchange

I'm sure Petrosian had missed he was making this switch possible by opening the 4th rank with 32.e5. Now it's a bit desperate!
34.♖g1 ♖xg1+ 35.♔xg1 ♕h5 36.f6 ♕g4+ 37.♕g3 ♖d7 38.♕xg4 ♗xg4 39.♘e4

39...h6
Petrosian gets lucky! 39...♖d5 was the way to do it, making sure the rook stays active.

40.♘d6

Now the black rook is dominated and White is out of danger.

40...♗e6 41.b3 a5 42.♗e3 a4 43.bxa4 ♖a7 44.♘e4 ♖b7 45.♘xc5 ♖b1+ 46.♔f2 ♖b2+ 47.♔g1 ♔f7 48.♗d4 ♖xa2 49.♘b7 ♔e8 50.♘c5 ♔f7 Draw.

This is a typically thorough effort from the Greek GM on an instructive topic. Definitely worth a look! 4 stars!

■ ■ ■

We round off with *Trompowsky Attack & London System* by Viktor Moskalenko (New In Chess). I can't say that these openings would necessarily be ones to get my pulse racing but Moskalenko has his own unique presentation style which never fails to catch your attention in some way. PUZZLE! WEAPON! TRICK! PLAN! These words accompanied by a shaded text box liven up the narrative, alerting you to a tactic or a key idea. Moskalenko's chess style is very inventive – he always has lots of little ideas in every type of position whatever the opening – and this presentation style dovetails very nicely with his chess style. I always discover something new when browsing through, and this game was one of them. It all looks so simple, it makes you want to try it!

**Kirill Shevchenko
Arjun Erigaisi**
Chess.com Junior Speed 2021 (final 1)
London System

1.d4 ♘f6 2.♗f4 e6 3.♘f3 c5 4.e3 ♘c6 5.c3 d5 6.♘bd2 cxd4

6...♘h5 'WEAPON!', says Moskalenko! 7.♗g5 f6 8.♗h4 g6 9.g4 ♘g7 10.♗g3 ♗d6 11.dxc5 ♗xc5 12.e4 with a complex struggle.

7.exd4 ♘h5

'A modern concept but there are already 900 games with it. After removing the "London bishop" from the b8-h2 diagonal, Black will be looking for a better place for his dark-squared bishop.'

8.♗e3 ♗d6 9.♗d3

'A solid strategy. Both these young grandmasters know how to play the London System. Moreover, this line was repeated three times in their online blitz match. The Ukrainian played the line with White and confidently showed better preparation, easily outplaying his opponent from the opening'

9.♘e5. Moskalenko also points out this WEAPON! '9...g6 10.g4 ♘g7 11.h4 h5 (11...♘xe5 may be a bit risky 12.dxe5 ♗xe5 13.h5) 12.♗g5 ♕b6 13.♗f6 ♖g8. This could be a very critical position. The solution for White is very concrete: 14.g5 ♘xe5 15.dxe5 ♗c5 16.♕f3 ♕xb2 17.♖b1

Moskalenko's chess style is very inventive – he always has lots of little ideas in every type of position whatever the opening

♕xa2 and now 18.♗c4 with the idea 18...dxc4 (18...♕a5 19.0-0) 19.♖xb7, winning. It is clear that these analyses should be checked for both sides with great care!'

9...♘f4 10.♗xf4 ♗xf4 11.0-0 0-0 12.♖e1

'Not many games were played in this position – 25 in total. White's results are positive, mainly because he

Trompowsky Attack & London System
Viktor Moskalenko
New In Chess, 2022
★★★★☆

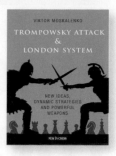

controls the centre, which allows him to play on both flanks.'

12...f6 13.b4

'In all three games of the match, Shevchenko started with this advance. 13.♕c2 WEAPON! contains a little trick: 13...g6 14.♗xg6 hxg6 15.♕xg6+. White captures the bishop on f4 with ♕h5+ and ♕g4+.'

13...♕d6 14.g3 ♗h6 15.b5 ♘e7 16.c4

'White is clearly better.'

16...♗d7

'16...dxc4 17.♘xc4.'

17.c5 ♕c7 18.a4 ♖ae8 19.♘b3 g6

20.♗f1

20.a5 is even stronger, according to Moskalenko. White clearly has a fantastic position and managed to put Black away in this blitz game.

20...♗g7 21.♗h3 ♘f5 22.♖c1 ♔h8 23.c6 bxc6 24.♘c5 ♗c8 25.♘d3 ♘d6 26.♖xc6 ♕d8 27.♘c5 f5 28.♘e5 ♘e4 29.♘cd3 ♗b7 30.♖c2 ♕b6 31.♘f4 g5 32.♘h5 ♗xe5 33.dxe5 f4 34.g4 d4 35.♗g2 ♘c3 36.♖xc3 ♗xg2 37.♔xg2 dxc3 38.♕d7 f3+ 39.♔g1 ♖g8 40.♘f6 1-0.

An opening book packed with tempting ideas! 4 stars! ■

Jan Timman

Rook around the clock

Rook endings are frequently on the menu for every chess player. They are tricky and can earn or cost you points. Even at the highest level. Jan Timman draws lessons from instructive rook endings from the Tata Steel Chess Tournament.

The 85th Tata Steel Chess Tournament saw a number of rook endings that attracted widespread attention and led to lively discussions and analysis. In most cases there were seven pieces on the board at the point where they became interesting. As a result, any mistake by a player could immediately be spotted by the available table base (today's most advanced table base has the 'solution' to all endings with a maximum of seven pieces – a piece being any piece or pawn. For the moment an 8-piece table base remains a pipe dream as the numbers involved are astronomical – ed.).

Yet, plenty questions were left unanswered. In his introduction to *Secrets of Rook Endings*, John Nunn wrote: 'The human author (has; …) to act as an interpreter. All the computer can do is say which moves win and how long the win will take. It cannot explain why some moves win and other, apparently similar, do not. It is also unable to derive characteristic themes which occur time and again.'

This was in 1992 and concerned rook endings with only one pawn.

These days, we've come to understand rook endings with three pawns. It has struck me that the endgames Nunn dealt with were often harder to fathom than those with two extra pawns. This seems paradoxical, but it is not uncommon in chess that positions get more difficult as fewer pieces are left. Rook endings with just one pawn are very abstract; with two more pawns, you start recognising patterns and identifying positions you can work towards.

I'll start with an endgame from the Challengers. This was the only game that Alexander Donchenko, the winner of the Challengers, lost.

John Nunn wrote: 'The computer cannot explain why some moves win and other, apparently similar, do not'

Alexander Donchenko
Erwin l'Ami
Wijk aan Zee Challengers 2023 (9)

position after 50...♖xb2

White is a pawn down, but as long he as he manages to hang on to his e-pawn, he won't be in danger of losing, since the white king will stay 'stuck' to the black pawn.
51.♔b7 f6 52.♔c6 ♔e6 53.♔c7 ♖b5! A devious move. White should be very careful now.

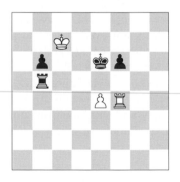

54.♔c6?
White has underestimated the danger. He should have prevented Black's next move with 54.♖h4!, after which Black cannot make effective progress, as witness:
– 54...♖b4. Threatening ...♔e5 and forcing White to withdraw his rook: 55.♖f4. If Black advances his king, he will save his skin (again) with a check on f5.
– 54...♖g5 55.♔xb6 ♔e5 56.♔c5 (incidentally, White could also have drawn with 56.♔c6, or even 56.♔c7, intending to attack the black pawn from behind) 56...♖g3 57.♔c4 ♖e3

ANALYSIS DIAGRAM

and now, 58.♖h6! is the only rook move; otherwise Black's king would capture on e4. After 58...♖xe4+ 59.♔d3 f5 60.♖h1 (or 60.♖h2) White has reached a theoretically drawn position.
54...♖h5! 55.♔xb6 ♔e5
The decisive tempo.

In the last round Alexander Donchenko avenged his earlier loss in a rook endgame against Erwin l'Ami as he defeated Velimir Ivic from a drawish rook ending.

56.♖f1 56.♖g4 would have been met decisively by 56...♖h3, followed by ...♖e3.
56...♖h4 57.♖f5+ ♔e6
White resigned.

Lesson learned
For the defender: make sure that your rook always has sufficient elbow room, and anticipate your opponent's plans.

Donchenko showed great resilience after his only defeat, bouncing back with four consecutive wins. In the final round, he avenged his defeat at the hands of l'Ami, winning a drawn rook ending. The roles had been reversed.

Alexander Donchenko
Velimir Ivic
Wijk aan Zee Challengers 2023 (13)

position after 39...♔f5

This is an endgame with more than seven pieces, but not an overly complicated one. White is a pawn up, but if Black stays alert, White has no real winning chances.
40.h5 ♖a1+ The infamous 40th move! With simply 40...♔g5, the draw would have been preserved; swapping the white h-pawn for the black g-pawn becomes inevitable.
41.♔h2 g6 The idea behind the previous move. But now White springs an unpleasant surprise.

42.g4+! Creating a strong passed pawn. **42...♔g5** The alternative 42...♔xg4 would have made no difference: after 43.hxg6 ♖a8 44.♖h3 (or 44.♖f7) White will win easily.
43.♖g7 Forcing Black to capture the g-pawn. **43...♔xg4 44.h6!**

With the rook on g7, White does not take back the g-pawn.
44...♜a8 45.♖xg6+ ♚f5 46.♖g7 ♜h8 47.h7 The rest is simple.

47...♚e4 48.♚g3 ♚xd4 49.♚f4 ♚d3 50.♖e7 d4 51.♚f5 ♚c2 52.♚xf6 d3 53.♚g7 d2 54.♖c7+ Black resigned.

Lesson learned

For the defender: when offering a pawn swap, start by ascertaining that your opponent has no unexpected move to create a dangerous passed pawn.

In the top group, the Tata Steel Masters, three rook endings got tongues wagging. In the penultimate round, Gukesh almost managed to inflict Aronian's first defeat.

Gukesh D
Levon Aronian
Wijk aan Zee Masters 2023 (12)

position after 52...♚xh5

White has two connected passed pawns that would normally win against Black's single one.
But here the black g-pawn is more

In case of a pawn race on opposite wings, it is very important to calculate as accurately as possible, and not to depend on general guidelines

advanced and is supported by its king.
53.a4 White's best practical chance.
53...♖f3 54.♖h7+ ♚g6 Black needs the tempo gained by attacking the white rook. After 54...♚g5 55.a5 the white passed pawn will decide.
55.♖h1

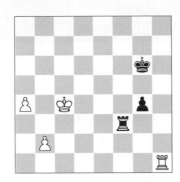

55...♖f4+! Quite correct; Black must start giving rook checks.
56.♚b5 ♖f5+ 57.♚b4 ♖f4+ 58.♚a3 g3 59.♖g1

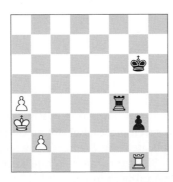

59...♖g4
An instructive mistake. One of the principles in rook endings is to put the rook behind the passed pawn. But this only applies to the attacking player. As a rule, the defender should give his rook a free rein. With 59...♖f3+ Black could have secured a draw. While the

white king moves up the board, Black continues to check it, and 60.b3 will be followed by 60...♚f7 61.a5 ♚e7.

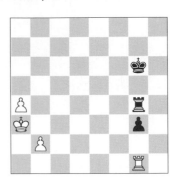

60.a5 The wrong pawn! It's usually a good idea to advance the foremost passed pawn, but not here. The correct move was 60.b4, the point of which becomes clear after 60...♚f7 61.b5 ♚e7 62.b6 ♚d7. Now the black king is cut off by 63.♖c1!. Black is powerless in the face of the white passed pawns. There could still follow: 63...g2 64.b7 ♖g3+ 65.♚a2 ♖g8 66.a5, and the a-pawn will be in time.
60...♚f7 61.b4 ♚e7 62.a6 ♚d7 63.a7 ♖g8

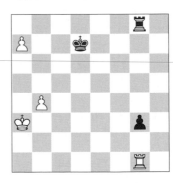

The black pieces have made a timely return to the defence.
64.♚a4 ♚c6 65.♖xg3 ♖h8 White is two pawns up, but has no winning chances. The white a-pawn has advanced too far and is too exposed.
66.♖g7 ♚b6 67.♚b3 ♖h3+ 68.♚c4 ♖h4+ 69.♚b3 ♖h3+ 70.♚a4 ♖h8 71.♖h7 ♖a8 72.♖f7

Lesson learned

For the attacker: in case of a pawn race on opposite wings, it is very important to calculate as accurately as possible, and not to depend on general guidelines.

For the defender: keep your rook's options as open as you can.

Vincent Keymer was the only player who didn't manage to win a game. Twice he came close. In Round 9 he allowed Abdusattorov, who was leading at the time, to slip the net. In their rook ending, Keymer missed a win no fewer than four times. But then, the deceptively simple-looking endgame was actually quite complicated.

Vincent Keymer
Nodirbek Abdusattorov
Wijk aan Zee Masters 2023 (9)

Vincent Keymer learned a few rook endgame lessons the hard way as he failed to convert promising positions against Nodirbek Abdusattorov and Jorden van Foreest.

position after 55...♖b4

It starts with eight pieces. The position is more difficult than it appears.
56.♖h5+ Confronting Black with a difficult choice: should the king advance or retreat?
56...♔d4?
The wrong choice. With 56...♔e6 (or 56...♔d6) Black could have held the endgame. After 57.♖f5 d4 58.♖xf4 ♖a4 59.♖e4+ ♔d5 White cannot really make progress.
57.♖h8?
White fails to take his chance. The obvious move was 57.♖f5!, cornering Black. The black king blocks the d-pawn and can no longer return. The main line continues as follows: 57...♔c4 58.g5 d4 59.g6 ♖b8 60.♔xf4 d3 61.♔e3!, and the white king stops the d-pawn, allowing the white passed pawns to decide.

57...♔e5! Well played. The king is back defending.
58.♖e8+ ♔f6 59.♖f8+ ♔g6
Another mistake. Black's king should not have strayed too far from the d-pawn. Correct was 59...♔e5, reverting to the aforementioned line.

60.♖f5
And again, White fails to pounce. He should have attacked the black d-pawn with 60.♖d8!, after which Black will slowly but surely be out-manoeuvred. After 60...♖d4 61.♖e8 Black has the following options:
– 61...♔f6 62.♖f8+ ♔e5 63.♖f5+ ♔e6 64.♖xf4, and this reveals the difference with other lines; the black took blocks the d-pawn, making Black's position hopeless.
– 61...♖a4 62.♖e6+ (not 62.♖e5, in view of 62...d4, and Black will get away) 62...♔f7 63.♖d6 ♖d4 64.g5!, with a curious situation. Materially, the players are equal, and Black seems to be in no serious danger. Yet his position is hopelessly lost, for example: 64...♖d2 65.♖f6+ ♔g7 66.♖xf4 ♔g6 67.♔g4, and everything is clear.
60...d4 61.♖d5
If White captures the pawn on f4, that is now unprotected after Black's pawn push, Black will force a draw: 61.♖xf4 ♖b3+ 62.♔e2 ♖b4 (or 62...♖b2+) 63.♔d3 ♖b3+ 64.♔xd4 ♔g5 65.♖e4 ♖f3, and the f-pawn will fall.
61...♔f6 62.♔e4

Another critical moment: which pawn to advance for Black to get counterplay?

62...d3+

And this was the wrong one. With the not-so-obvious 62...f3, Black could have saved the game by making use of White's efforts to win the f-pawn. There could follow: 63.♖f5+ ♔e6 64.♖e5+ ♔f6 65.g5+ ♔g6, and White will be unable to make progress.

63.♔f3 Not 63.♔xd3, of course, in view of 63...f3, with a draw.

63...♔e6 64.♖xd3 ♔e5 65.♖a3 ♖b5 66.♔g2 ♔f6

67.♖a8 White could have won with 67.♖h3!, the idea being to keep the black king from g5 and meet 67...♖b2 with 68.♖h5, and White will encircle the f-pawn.

67...♖b3

Cutting off the white king is a good idea in itself, but Black shouldn't have given up the fifth rank. With 67...♔g5! Black would have held. It may look as if White then has 68.♖g8+ ♔h4 69.♔f3, winning the f-pawn, but Black continues 69...♖b3+ 70.♔xf4 ♖b4+ 71.♔f3 ♖b3+ 72.♔g2 ♖b2!. Such endgames with two connected passed pawns are usually won, unless the pawns are blocked. This is not the case here, but the activity of the black pieces still stops White's progress.

68.♖a5! Now White manages to encircle the f-pawn after all.

68...♔g6 69.♖f5 ♖a3

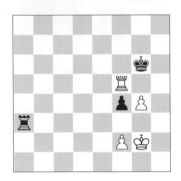

70.f3 Well played. White couldn't take the pawn, since 70.♖xf4 ♔g5 71.♖b4 ♔h4! would have led to another such exceptional position in which Black will draw: after 72.f3 ♖a2+ 73.♔f1 ♔g3 White would need to have his rook on f5 to win.

70...♖a4 71.♔h3 ♖b4 72.♔h4 ♖a4 73.♖f8 ♔g7 74.♖f5 ♔g6 75.♖g5+ ♔h7 76.♖h5+ ♔g6 77.g5 ♖a1 78.♖h6+ ♔f5 79.♖f6+ ♔e5

80.♖b6 White's final error. Here, he should have cut off the black king with 80.♖f8, or even 80.♖f7. The former move is obviously winning, but with the rook on f7, things are

YOUNG GRANDMASTERS HAVE THEIR OWN SPECIFIC FEARS

SLEEP WELL MY SON, THERE IS NO FISCHER, KASPAROV OR CARLSEN UNDER YOUR BED

BEREND VONK

VONK

not immediately clear. The following line illustrates this: 80...♖h1+ 81.♔g4 ♖g1+ 82.♔h5 ♖g3 83.♔g6 ♖xf3, and now White cuts off the black king with 84.♖e7+. After 84...♔d6 85.♖e4 or 84...♔d5 85.♔f5 the black f-pawn becomes useless: it is dominated by the white pieces, and the g-pawn's road is cleared. It is important here that the black king stays cut off to prevent it from supporting the f-pawn.

80...♖h1+ 81.♔g4 ♖g1+ 82.♔h5 ♖g3 Now the situation has changed, because the black king is not cut off. A draw is inevitable.

83.♖b3 ♔f5 84.♖b5+ ♔e6 85.g6 ♖xf3 86.g7 ♖g3 87.♔h6 f3 88.♖b8 ♖h3+ 89.♔g6 Draw.

Lesson learned

For the attacker: always choose the best, most active square for the rook, and if you have a passed pawn, do your damnedest to cut off the enemy king.

For the defender: keep your defence as compact as you can and in emergencies, rather aim for positions two pawns down but with active pieces than positions one pawn down and restricted activity.

In the next round, Keymer got another rook ending one pawn up, forcing him again to work well into the evening. And again the 18-year-old German GM found himself robbed.

Jorden van Foreest
Vincent Keymer
Wijk aan Zee Masters 2023 (10)

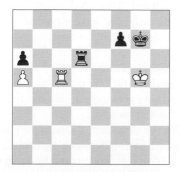

position after 47.♔xg5

This endgame seems pretty drawish, despite Black's extra pawn. White is very active, and it seems impossible for Black to chase him from the fifth rank. Yet the position is problematic for White, since only Black has the possibility to make progress.

47...♖f6 48.♔g4 ♔f8 49.♔g5 ♖d6 50.♔f5 ♔e7 51.♔e4 ♖e6+ 52.♔f4 ♔d7 53.♖f5 f6

Black has made progress, and the position has turned critical for White.

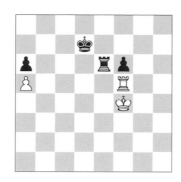

54.♖h5?

A passive move really. White could no longer keep his rook on the fifth rank, so 54.♖d5+ was called for, intending to meet 54...♔c6 with 55.♖d8. After 55...♔b5 56.♖d5+ ♔b4 the rook returns with 57.♖f5!. This rook manoeuvre is somewhat surprising, but well-founded. With the black king unable to return, White is in no danger of losing his control of the fifth rank.

54...♔c6

Obvious enough, and Keymer played it immediately. But it let the win slip. He should have activated his rook with 54...♖e1 or 54...♖e2. If White checks on h7, the black king goes to c6, while 55.♖h6 is met by 55...♔e6. In the end, White will lose his a-pawn without managing to manoeuvre his king into a very active position.

55.♖f5

White also fails to find the correct move. He should have left his rook passive and made his king active. Correct was 55.♖h1 (or 55.♖h2) to take the rook to the a-file. White meets 55...♔b5 with 56.♔f5! ♖d6

57.♖a1, and White's king is so active that Black will be unable to make progress.

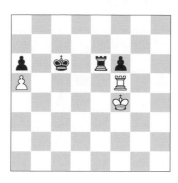

55...♔d6!

Now Keymer finds the correct plan: taking square d5 away from the white rook and exploiting the poor coordination of the white pieces.

56.♔f3

There's nothing else. White had to withdraw his king, since after 56.♖h5 ♖e5 57.♖h6 ♔e6 Black would win immediately.

56...♔e7 57.♔f4 ♖e1 58.♖h5 ♔d6 59.♖h2 ♖e5 60.♖d2+ ♔e6 61.♖a2

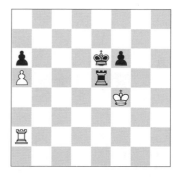

The situation is now very different from in the line I gave after White's 55th move.

61...♖f5+ 62.♔g4 ♖d5 63.♖a1 ♖d4+ 64.♔h5 ♖e4 65.♖a2 ♖e1 66.♔g4 f5+ Finally, after endless hesitation, Black advances his passed pawn. Nor was there any reason to postpone it any longer. But Black will have to be very careful now.

67.♔f3 ♖e5 The final error, which eventually caused Keymer to leave

Wijk aan Zee without a single victory. Correct was 67...♔e5. Black needs to gain as much ground as possible to round off the game.

68.♖a4!
Excellent play. White doesn't give his opponent any chance to redress his error. Now the fourth rank is under his control, making square f4 available to the white king. From here on in, Van Foreest plays faultlessly. It seems as if he had initially underestimated the dangers in this endgame.
68...♖b5 69.♔f4
Again the only move.
69...♔d6 70.♖a1 ♖c5

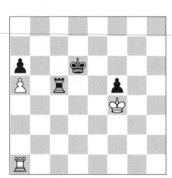

Now White must be careful.
71.♖b1!
The only move; Black was threatening to take his king to b5 via c6.
71...♖xa5 72.♖b6+ ♔c5

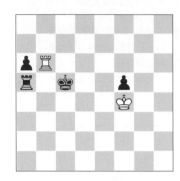

73.♖f6!
Certainly not 73.♖e6, in view of 73...♖a1 74.♔xf5 a5, and Black wins because the white king remains cut off. The text leads to a theoretical draw which – in a slightly different form – is known from the game Smyslov-Bondarevsky, Moscow 1940.
73...♔c4 74.♖c6+ ♔b5 75.♖f6 ♖a4+ 76.♔f3

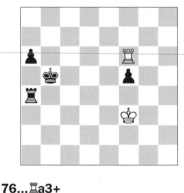

76...♖a3+

Now White will win the f-pawn by force without his king remaining cut off. After 76...f4 77.♖f5+ a draw would also be inevitable; on the next move, White will capture on f4.
77.♔e2 ♖a2+ 78.♔e1 ♖a1+ 79.♔e2 ♖a2+ 80.♔e1 ♖c2 81.♖xf5+ ♔b4 82.♔d1 ♖c4 83.♖f8 a5 84.♖b8+ ♔a3 85.♖b5 a4 86.♔d2 ♔a2 87.♖b8 ♖h4 88.♔c2 ♖h2+ 89.♔c1 a3 90.♖b7 ♖b2 91.♖c7 ♖b6 92.♖c2+

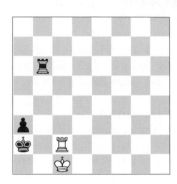

White could also have kept his rook on c8, but Van Foreest has planned a nice finale.
92...♔a1 93.♖c3 ♔a2 94.♖c2+ ♔b3 95.♔b1 ♖d6

96.♖b2+! The final point. Draw. White could also have played his rook to c1, of course.

Lesson learned
For the attacker: try to gain space and have good coordination between king and rook.
For the defender: also aim for good coordination between your pieces, and don't underestimate the dangers in drawish-looking positions. ∎

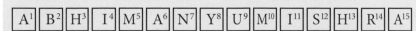

They are The Champions

EMMANUEL JIMÉNEZ
Costa Rica

For some chess players, winning a national title might be enough to satisfy them. Not Emmanuel Jiménez of Costa Rica. The 26-year-old International Master says that his clinching the top spot in the Costa Rica Championship in January was just another achievement that brings him closer to his ultimate goal: becoming a grandmaster.

'I'm happy to have won the tournament, but right now I feel like I'm just riding a wave of momentum that will hopefully bring me to where I want to be in terms of my chess goals,' Jiménez said.

In the Costa Rican championship, which was held between January 7 and 15 in San José, Jiménez went head-to-head with some of his country's best players. Though he remained undefeated, he won the event by a narrow margin, edging out the defending 2022 champion by only half a point.

'It was close, so the victory was really rewarding', Jiménez said.

Even so, Jiménez didn't spend much time basking in the glory of his win. In fact, on the day after the tournament finished, he and his chess coach spent hours analysing games and planning out which 2023 tournaments will make the most sense to play.

In **They are The Champions** we pay tribute to national champions across the globe. For suggestions please write to editors@newinchess.com.

Jiménez, who already has one grandmaster norm, hopes not only to be a grandmaster, but also to crack 2600 and perhaps even make it into the top 100 players in the world.

Such goals may sound lofty, but they may also be well timed.

Currently, Costa Rica does not have an active grandmaster, and, Jiménez says, its chess community is having problems with something called 'generational relief'. Basically, he says, many of the country's top players are retiring, and there haven't been enough younger players of similar strength to replace them. Why this problem exists isn't exactly known, but Jiménez hopes that by achieving the grandmaster title, he will attract more attention to chess and motivate more players, too.

Certainly, if he continues to play as resourcefully as he did in the following game from the national championship, he will soon reach his goal.

Sergio Duran Vega
Emmanuel Jiménez Garcia
Costa Rica Championship 2023

position after 28...c4

Black's last move was a mistake.
29.axb5 But White fails to spot that he could get a winning attack with 29.♕h5 ♘f7 30.♕f5 ♔h8 31.axb5 axb5 32.♖f1.
29... ♕xb5 30.♕d2

After this mistake (he should have played 30.♘g5+) Black strikes.
30...♖xg3+! 31.♖xg3 ♖xg3+ 32.♔h2 ♘xe4 Clearly thrown off balance, White makes a number of errors that lead to his demise.
33.♕c2 ♕xd5 34.♘c5 ♖g4 35.♖e1 ♕f7 36.♖e3 This leads to a forced mate, but White was lost anyway.
36...♕f4+ and before he got mated, White resigned. ∎

Jonathan Tisdall

CURRENT ELO: Around 2400

DATE OF BIRTH: August 26, 1958

PLACE OF BIRTH: Buffalo, NY, USA

PLACE OF RESIDENCE: Asker, Norway

What is your favourite city?
It's been taking a beating lately, but I would still have to say London.

What was the last great meal you had?
This is very easy, a multi-course gourmet feast at Oogst in The Hague, with Dirk Jan and Remmelt from New In Chess.

What drink brings a smile to your face?
A fine gin and tonic.

Which book would you give to a friend?
The Unconsoled by Kazuo Ishiguro. Despite being totally surreal, to me it somehow magically describes the life of a travelling performer.

What book are you currently reading?
A Kindle, currently displaying *The Book of Accidents* by Chuck Wendig.

What is your all-time favourite movie?
Francois Truffaut's *Day for Night* convinced me to study film at university.

And your favourite TV series?
For now I'll say *Breaking Bad*.

Do you have a favourite actor?
It used to be young Jack Nicholson, lately I've been impressed by Tom Hardy.

And a favourite actress?
I can always count on Helen Mirren.

What music do you listen to?
I literally listen to every 'genre', but right now 'indie' is in – Camera Obscura and Japanese Breakfast.

Is there a work of art that moves you?
I'm very partial to Ukiyo-e and Impressionism.

Who is your all time favourite player?
Probably Kasparov, because I spent so much time watching many of his pivotal performances, live. And because of the energy in his games.

Is there a chess book that had a profound influence on you?
Have to go all the way back to the indoctrination stage, and say *The Fireside Book of Chess* by Chernev and Reinfeld.

What was your best result ever?
Probably 1= at the Reykjavik Open in ... 1995? A GM performance clinched two rounds before the end was pretty unusual for me...

And the best game you played?
Flashiest is the 1981 miniature vs. Edward Lee, but as a whole, maybe Black vs. Øgaard from Gausdal 1987.

What was the most exciting chess game you ever saw?
Kasparov-Karpov, Game 24, Seville.

Do chess players have typical shortcomings?
No, all shortcomings are possible.

Facebook, Instagram, Snapchat, or?
Twitter. But I use them all to some degree.

Who do you follow on Twitter?
All sorts. Too many. And there are three of me.

What is your life motto?
Try to be kind, and never grow up.

When were you happiest?
When my children were young enough to joke around with constantly.

Who or what would you like to be if you weren't yourself?
A successful/contented musician of some kind.

What is the best piece of advice you were ever given?
Here's my favourite Harpo Marx quote: 'Many years ago a very wise man named Bernard Baruch took me aside (..). "Harpo my boy," he said, "I'm going to give you three pieces of advice, three things you should always remember." My heart jumped and I glowed with expectation (..). "Yes sir?" I said. And he told me the three things. I regret that I've forgotten what they were."

Is there something you'd love to learn?
A major language; some form of Chinese or Arabic.

What would people be surprised to know about you?
I spend a lot of time with stand-up comedians.

If you could change one thing in the chess world, what would it be?
Erase engines.

What does it mean to be a chess player?
Being independent.

Is a knowledge of chess useful in everyday life?
Not directly, but I believe thinking hard is good for you.

What is the best thing that was ever said about chess?
I regret that I've forgotten what it was.